OUTSTANDING STORIES
by PAST
GENERAL
AUTHORITIES

OUTSTANDING STORIES *by* PAST GENERAL AUTHORITIES

compiled by
LEON R. HARTSHORN

spring creek
BOOK COMPANY

Provo, Utah

Copyright © 2007 Leon R. Hartshorn

All Rights Reserved.

This book is not an official publication of The Church of Jesus Christ of Latter-day Saints.

ISBN: 978-1-932898-58-3
e. 2

Published by:
Spring Creek Book Company
P.O. Box 50355
Provo, Utah 84605-0355
www.springcreekbooks.com

Cover design © Spring Creek Book Company

Printed in the United States of America
10 9 8 7 6 5 4 3 2 1
Printed on acid-free paper

Library of Congress Cataloging-in-Publication Data

Outstanding stories by general authorities.
   Outstanding stories by past general authorities / compiled by Leon R. Hartshorn.
   p. cm.
   Originally published: Original stories by general authorities. Salt Lake City : Deseret Book Co., 1970-1973.
   Includes bibliographical references.
   ISBN 978-1-932898-58-3 (pbk. : alk. paper)
   1. Mormons--Biography. 2. Church officers--Biography. I. Hartshorn, Leon R. II. Title.

BX8693.O97 2007
289.3092'2--dc22
[B]
                                     2006100031

TABLE OF CONTENTS

JOSEPH ANDERSON 1
   Give Heber $10,000 2

MARVIN J. ASHTON 4
   I'll Never Get in Anyone's Way 5
   He Is An Old Grouch Today 5
   A Silver Dollar in My Hand 6
   He's For Sale Pretty Cheap 7

EZRA TAFT BENSON 8
   Well, What You Want Is a Returned Mormon Missionary 9
   More Loyal Support for One Another 10
   Separation for a Period of Two Years 11
   That Was President Smith 12
   They Just Stood There and Visited and Visited 13
   Twenty-Two People Were Living in One Room 14
   From Somewhere They Had Obtained an Old Radio 15
   Many of These Saints Dressed in Rags 17

HUGH B. BROWN 19
   I Went Around to the Back Door 20
   When the Bell Rings 21
   Would Anyone Like to Undertake Such a Task? 22
   Send Us Water 23
   You Will Be Honorable 24
   Examination for Discovery 26
   No, I'm Not in Trouble 29
   Father, Are You There? 30
   I Only Touched Ground Once 31
   Thank You, God 34
   The Gardener and the Currant Bush 37

THEODORE M. BURTON 40
There's an Eagle in Your Chicken Yard 41
We Have Enough—Don't Bring Any More 43
I Had Found It in Mr. Goddard's Grocery Store 45

MATTHEW COWLEY 46
We Are Fasting and Praying 47
I'm Ready Now to Bless Your Boy 48
What on Earth Will I Do? 49
He Was an Unusual Boy 49
Fix Me Up, I Want to Go Home 50
Just As Miraculous As Raising the Dead 51
The Doctor Isn't Home 52
The Mortgage Is Paid Off 52
You Do Not Owe That Much Tithing 53
Then I Am Safe for Another Week 54
See What You Have Done For Me 54
I Received a Message 55
Medical Science Had Laid the Burden Down 56
Send for the Elders 57
Give Him His Vision 57

JAMES A. CULLIMORE 59
This Is Where You Are Supposed to Be 60
But If You Put Him in Cold Water. 61
The Sand Kept Getting into My Shoes 62
I Forgot to Tell You, But He Rose Again 62
It Was a Feeling That She Had 63
Beware of the Mormons 64

RICHARD L. EVANS 65
We Cannot Make a Blade of Grass 66
When I Have Said What I Know to Be True 67
I Was Sufficiently Interested 68
No Greater Mission 68
Because My Father Said So 69
That's Statistics for You 70
I Still Plant Cherry Trees 71

Sometimes I Do Things I Know I Shouldn't Do 71
The Spirit of All Truth 72

MARION D. HANKS 74
   Kneel Down, Son 75
   Say, Hanks, Do You Believe in Jesus Christ? 76
   Boy, We Really Have a Swell Bathroom, Haven't We? 77

HOWARD W. HUNTER 79
   There Is Danger in Looking Backward 80
   The Learning Process Lies Within 81
   It All Started From a Prayer That Night 82

SPENCER W. KIMBALL 85
   That First Tithing Receipt 86
   The Breaking of Day Has Found Me on My Knees 86
   You Will See Him Someday as a Great Leader 88
   The Story of Lazarus 89
   Guests of the Lord 90

LEGRAND RICHARDS 93
   Point to That Meetinghouse 94
   A Natural-born Liar 94
   The Book of Mormon in the Same Cover with the Bible 96
   I Decided to Trade the Dollar for Five Dollars 97
   The Angels Brought That Spirit 98
   Are There Any Mormons Living Around Here? 100
   Maybe the Lord Can Save Her, But I Cannot 101
   I Am Afraid I Can't Answer That 102
   The Cart Before the Horse 103
   You Just Go On, and Live Right 104
   Mere Boy That I Was 105

STERLING W. SILL 107
   I Do Not Know What God Is 108
   You Can't Merely Snap Your Fingers 109
   A Black Walnut 110
   The Quicksands of His Own Mistakes 110
   This House Was His Wedding Present 111

I Just Don't Want Any Signboard Telling Me Where to Go 112
The "As If" Principle 112

ROBERT L. SIMPSON 114
Just a Few Pennies a Day 115
Charting a Course 116
The Game of Life 117
But Daddy, I Wasn't Talking to You 117
The Entire Maori Battalion 118
Chant of the Old Maoris 120
The Wyoming Cowboy 121
From the Mission Office 122

ELDRED G. SMITH 124
What a Patriarchal Blessing Can Do 125
I Met the Challenge 126
The Only Ones Sitting in the Audience 126
This Is Priesthood Order 129
Bishop, I See What You Came Here to Tell Me 130

N. ELDON TANNER 131
You and the Rest of the World 132
I Am Going to Report to the Lord Tonight 133
The Value of a Good Home 133
He Had Real Courage 134

HENRY D. TAYLOR 136
We Love One Another 137
Armchair Generals 137
Look at That Big Tree 139
Excess Baggage 140
He Received His First Paycheck 141
He Rebuked the Waves 142

A. THEODORE TUTTLE 143
Thank You 144
He Was Obviously from the Farm 144
A Young Boy's Answer 145
Let It Fly Clear up to the Sky 146

JOHN H. VANDENBERG...147
   The Most Wonderful Thing in the World......................................148
   My Dearest Father Bishopric 148

JOSEPH ANDERSON

Elder Joseph Anderson was born in Salt Lake City, Utah, on November 20, 1889. He graduated from Weber Academy, now Weber State College, at the age of 15.

He was a missionary for the Church in Switzerland and Germany from 1911 to 1914. He married Norma Peterson in the Salt Lake Temple on November 11, 1915. They have a son and two daughters.

After a brief business career in Salt Lake City, he became secretary to late Church President Heber J. Grant. He then served as the secretary to the First Presidency of the Church from 1923 to 1970. In this capacity he traveled throughout the world with the presidents of the Church on their various assignments.

He was sustained as Assistant to the Quorum of the Twelve Apostles in 1970, and then as a member of the First Quorum of the Seventy in 1976. He was granted emeritus status in 1978.

Elder Anderson passed away in Salt Lake City on March 13, 1992, at the age of 102.

Give Heber $10,000

There is another story I would like to tell you that President Grant often told. Whenever the Church needed someone to collect funds for some important purpose, they called on Brother Grant. At the time, of course, he was an apostle. And he was a great financier and a wonderful man for contributing to funds and for collecting funds. On one occasion, it so happened that one of the banks in Salt Lake was in trouble, and it looked like it might fail. Some of the Brethren were interested in the bank as directors, and if it had failed, it would have been quite an embarrassment to them. And the President of the Church called on Brother Grant to go out and collect funds that they might put into the bank to save it from disaster.

Now some people questioned the wisdom of that, but at any rate Brother Grant went forward on his mission. And one of the places he visited was Provo where he called on Jesse Knight and Reed Smoot. He asked Reed Smoot for $2,000, and he asked Jesse for $5,000. They were both men of means, Brother Knight particularly, as some of you well know.

Jesse wasn't altogether sold on the idea. He said, "No, I don't think that an apostle of the Lord ought to be going out gathering funds for that purpose. I don't think that that's a worthy cause to go out and make collections for."

And Brother Smoot said, "I'll give you $1,000, but I won't give you $2,000."

Brother Grant said, "Brother Smoot, you have offered $1,000. I'll not take it, but you go home tonight and get down on your knees and pray to the Lord and ask him to give you enlargement of the heart and give me $2,000."

Jesse said, "Brother Grant, why didn't you ask me to pray?"

"Oh," Brother Grant said, "why should I ask you to pray? You didn't offer me anything. No use of asking the Lord to give you enlargement of the heart."

Brother Knight had told him, "You can come here as often as you want, and there is a bed and breakfast for you at my home, but I'm not going to contribute to that." And he was a very generous contributor normally.

He said, "I'll tell you what I will do. I will go home tonight, and I will pray to the Lord about that. And if I get the inspiration to give you that $5,000, I'll do it."

"Well," Brother Grant said, "I might as well have the check in my pocket now. I am sure if you pray about it I'll get it."

And so, two or three days later there came through the mail two checks—one from Jesse M. Knight for $10,000, and one from Brother Smoot for $2,000.

When Brother Grant saw Jesse a few days later, he said, "What happened? I didn't ask you for $10,000. I only asked for $5,000."

Brother Knight said, "I'll tell you this, Brother Grant. When you come to me again with a mission from the President of the Church to raise funds, I'm going to pay without any question." He said, "You're much more liberal than the Lord is. I went home as I promised to do, and I told the Lord that Heber was asking me for this contribution, and I wanted to know how he felt about it. I got down on my knees, and it just kept going through my mind like a tune: 'Give Heber $10,000.' And I got into bed and that tune kept going through my mind: 'Give Heber $10,000. Give Heber $10,000.' I got down on my knees again and said, 'Lord, Heber didn't ask me for $10,000. He only asked for $5,000.' The tune kept going through my mind. 'Give Heber $10,000. Give Heber $10,000.' And so, in order to satisfy the situation and have peace of mind, I told the Lord, 'All right, I'll give him $10,000.'"

And so, that is what happened. This is one of the experiences of many that President Grant used to tell that were very interesting to me.

Brigham Young University, *Speeches of the Year*, "Prophets of the Living God," July 29, 1969, pp. 6-7.

MARVIN J. ASHTON

Elder Marvin J. Ashton was born in Salt Lake City on May 6, 1915, a son of Marvin O. and Rae J. Ashton. He graduated from the University of Utah in business administration and was married in the Salt Lake Temple in 1940 to Norma Berntson. They are the parents of four children.

He was ordained a member of the Quorum of Twelve Apostles on December 2, 1971. Throughout his life he directed much of his time and attention to youth leadership. He served as a national committeeman of the Boy Scouts of America, and received the Silver Bear and Silver Antelope Scouting awards for outstanding service to boys.

He served a Church mission in Great Britain from 1937 to 1939 and was captain of the missionary basketball team that won the British National championship.

During his service as an apostle, he traveled the world and was loved for his inspiring messages, gentle manner and warm smile.

Elder Ashton died February 25, 1994 in Salt Lake City.

I'll Never Get in Anyone's Way

Two weeks ago last Sunday we were in a stake conference. When it was time for the closing prayer, the stake president announced the individual's name who had been given the assignment. There were four verses in the closing song. At the beginning of the third verse I noticed a young man start from the audience, making his way to the pulpit to give the prayer. As he came toward the pulpit I noticed he was moving with a great deal of difficulty, and as he came even closer I could see that one leg was braced, heavily braced. He walked with a cane. He walked slowly. He walked with a great deal of effort as well as a great deal of courage. He barely made it to the pulpit before the song was over.

Just before he gave the benediction, the stake president nudged me and said, "This young man has just returned from the mission field." He said, "Just about two and one-half years ago he came to me after visiting with his bishop and said, 'I'd like to go on a mission. I know I have physical handicaps but I would like to go.'"

The stake president hesitated, wondering what to say to the young man. Finally the young man said, to press the point, "President, if you and the bishop will let me go on a mission, I promise you one thing."

The stake president said, "What is it?"

He said, "I promise you if you'll let me go, I'll never get in anyone's way."

He went on his mission and he came back. He served in the West Central States Mission and had the opportunity of baptizing forty-seven people in the state of Montana . . . because he wouldn't get in anyone's way. What a great individual.

Speeches of the Year, "Murmur Not," December 9, 1969, p. 5.

He Is An Old Grouch Today

Years ago while walking with a wise friend of mine, we passed one of his neighbors as he stood in the front yard of his home. My friend greeted the man with, "How are you, Bill? It's good to see you." To this greeting, Bill didn't even look up. He didn't even respond.

"He is an old grouch today, isn't he?" I snapped.

"Oh, he is always that way," my friend responded.

"Then why are you so friendly to him?" I asked.

"Why not?" responded my mature friend. "Why should I let him decide how I am going to act?"

I hope I will never forget the lesson of that evening. The important word was *act*. My friend acted toward people. Most of us react. At the time it was a strange attitude to me, because I was in grade school and following the practice of "if you speak to an acquaintance and he does not respond, that is the last time you have to bother," or "if someone shoves you on the school playground, you shove him back."

I have thought many times since this experience that many of us are perpetual reactors. We let other people determine our actions and attitudes. We let other people determine whether we will be rude or gracious, depressed or elated, critical or loyal, passive or dedicated.

Do you know people who are cool toward an acquaintance because last time they met she wasn't warm in her greeting? Do you know people who have quit praying to the Lord because he hasn't answered (so they think) their prayers of last month or last year? Do you know people who give up on others because they don't respond in the ways we think they should? Do you know people who fail to realize that Christ-like behavior patterns encourage us to be the same yesterday and forever?

The perpetual reactor is an unhappy person. His center of personal conduct is not rooted within himself, where it belongs, but in the world about him. Some of us on occasion seem to be standing on the sidelines waiting for someone to hurt, ignore, or offend us. We are perpetual reactors. What a happy day it will be when we can replace hasty reaction with patience and purposeful action.

Conference Report, October 1970, pp. 36-37.

A Silver Dollar in My Hand

What a thrill it was the other day to be visiting with one of our handsome full-time Navajo Indian missionaries when he said, "The main reason I'm on a mission today is because when I was a small boy, President Spencer W. Kimball came into our home, patted me on the head, placed a silver dollar in my hand, and said, 'Take this and start saving for a mission.'"

Wrapped up in that example of leadership are all of the important parts: recognition, encouragement, challenge, and example. To bring groups back, we must learn to lead the individual back through patience and love. Good leaders don't give up. Good parents don't give up. Good youth don't give up.

Conference Report, April 1970, p. 25.

He's For Sale Pretty Cheap

It is time for us to reaffirm the great truth that God's paths are straight. They not only provide safety, but they also lead to happiness and eternal progression.

Speaking of staying on the straight paths, I will never forget an experience I had with a friend in central Utah a few years ago. He had for his hobby mountain lion hunting. With other associates, dependable horses, guns, and well-trained dogs, he would seek to track the lions down, or tree them for capture. One day when I visited his place of business, he had a full-grown hunting dog tied to one of his sheds. "Isn't he a beauty?" I commented. He responded with "He's got to go. I can't be bothered with him."

"What's the problem?" I continued.

"Since he was a pup, I have trained him to track lions. He knows what I expect. The last time we were out on a three-day hunt, he took off after a deer, then a coyote, and finally some rabbits, and was gone the best part of a full day. He knows he must stay on the trail of the lion to be one of mine. Our business is mountain lions. Yep, he's for sale pretty cheap."

How often are we led from the right track by distractions like drugs that cross our paths? Do we sometimes seek the available "rabbit" when the big game is available up the path?

Conference Report, April 1971, p. 13.

EZRA TAFT BENSON

President Ezra Taft Benson became the thirteenth president of the Church of Jesus Christ of Latter-day Saints on November 10, 1985. During his presidency he emphasized daily scripture study, particularly of the Book of Mormon. His addresses focused on family, freedom, and the need for additional missionaries.

From 1933 to 1937, he was a member of the stake presidency of the Boise Stake in Idaho. The following year the stake was divided, and he served as president of the Boise Stake for two years.

He then moved to Washington, D.C., where he became the first president of the Washington Stake, comprising all members of the Church near the nation's capital. He held this position until he was called to serve in the Council of the Twelve Apostles on October 7, 1943.

President Benson is a great-grandson of Ezra T. Benson, one of the original pioneers who entered the Salt Lake Valley with Brigham Young on July 24, 1947. His parents were among the early settlers of Southern Idaho, where in the small town of Whitney he was born August 4, 1899.

From 1921 to 1923, he served as a missionary in the British Isles. Following his return home, he continued his education at Brigham Young

University at Provo, Utah, where he was graduated with honors and given a scholarship to Iowa State College at Ames, Iowa. At this institution he received his M.S. degree and was elected to the Honor Society of Agriculture.

In 1946, he was appointed President of the European Mission of the Church with headquarters in London. The European members under local leadership had been carrying on during the war under distressing circumstances. Elder Benson was sent to attend to the spiritual affairs of the people, to reopen the missions, and to alleviate suffering among members.

U.S. President Dwight D. Eisenhower appointed him to his cabinet as Secretary of Agriculture in 1952, where he served until 1961.

He was married to Flora Smith Amussen and they are the parents of two sons and four daughters.

President Benson died on May 30, 1994 in Salt Lake City.

Well, What You Want Is A Returned Mormon Missionary

My brothers and sisters, as I travel about the world, it is a glorious thing to note how the Church is growing and increasing. One very fine leader of a foreign state, when I asked him if there were any Mormons in his particular capital city, said: "Mr. Secretary, I have traveled a great deal, and I have come to believe that the Mormons are everywhere. Wherever I go, I find them." His statement called to mind an incident when we first moved to Washington back in 1939 or 1940. I had gone to my office early to get some work done before the telephones started ringing. I had just seated myself at the desk when the telephone rang. The man at the other end said, "I would like to have lunch with you today. I am a stranger to you, but I have something that is very urgent." I consented reluctantly, and a few hours later we faced each other across a luncheon table at a downtown hotel.

He said, "I suppose you wonder why I have invited you here." Then he added: "Last week as I came out of a luncheon meeting in Chicago, I told some of my business associates that I had been given the responsibility of coming down to Washington, D. C., to establish an office and employ a man to represent our corporation."

Then he listed some of the assets in his great business organization. He said, "I began telling my associates of the kind of young man I would like to represent us in this office in Washington. First of all, I said to my associates, I wanted a man who is honest, a man of real integrity, a man who lives a clean life, who is clean morally, who, if married, is a devoted husband, and who, if unmarried, is not chasing lewd women."

He said, "I would like a man who doesn't drink, and if possible I would prefer to get a man who doesn't even smoke. One of my business associates spoke up and said, 'Well, what you want is a returned Mormon missionary.' I had heard of your Church," he said. "In fact, I recall two young men in dark suits calling at our home some months ago. As I rode down here on the train last night, I decided that maybe a returned Mormon missionary was exactly what I needed. Why not? So as I registered at the hotel last night I said to the man at the desk, 'Are there any Mormons in Washington?' And the man at the desk said, 'I don't know, I suppose there are. They seem to be everywhere. But Mr. Bush, the manager, is here, and I'll ask him.' He asked Mr. Bush and gave me your name. Now that is why I have invited you here. Can you give me the names of three or four young men who meet the standards which I have just outlined?"

Well, of course it was not difficult to give him the names of three or four or a dozen who fully met the standards he outlined. I mention this, my brethren and sisters and friends, because in the Church we have certain standards—standards of living, standards of morality, standards of character which are coming to be well-known to the world. These standards are admired. People with such standards are sought after. These standards are based upon true, eternal principles. They are eternal verities.

Conference Report, April 1958, pp. 59-60.

More Loyal Support for One Another

Some months ago while attending a meeting of agricultural and farm cooperative leaders in an eastern city, I had occasion to leave my hotel room and cross the street to the nearby post office to mail some letters. As I entered the door of the post office on a side street, I heard words coming through an open window at the opposite side of the building which sounded very much to me like a Mormon missionary preaching on the street.

After mailing the letters, I eased over to the open window, and there I saw two young men in blue serge suits standing on the corner of the steps of the post office. One young man was bearing his testimony regarding the coming forth of the Book of Mormon and the mission of the Prophet Joseph. He was earnest, he was sincere, he spoke with conviction. I thrilled with what he said. Some fifty or seventy-five people were listening in addition to the moving congregation that is always part of the street meeting. Standing at his side was his companion. In one arm were copies of the Book of Mormon, and the hats of the two brethren in his other hand.

When the street meeting ended, I went out and introduced myself, visited with them a moment, and then I turned to the young man who had been holding the literature in his arm and said, "Elder, what were you doing while your companion was preaching and bearing testimony?" The answer filled my soul with thanksgiving. He said, "Brother Benson, I was praying to God that my companion would say the right thing that would touch the hearts of the people and bring them a conviction of the truth of this great latter-day work."

Support for one another—that is the one thought that I have to leave with you, my brethren and sisters. One of our great needs as a people is greater, more loyal support for one another.

Conference Report, October 1951, pp. 154-55.

Separation for a Period of Two Years

I shall ever be grateful for an experience which came into our family during this latter period that I refer to, something over thirty years ago. It was during the time when sacrament meetings were held on Sunday afternoon at two o'clock, at least in the rural wards. I remember very well this particular Sunday afternoon, as father and mother returned from sacrament meeting, in the one-horse buggy.

As they drove into the yard and their little brood of seven kiddies gathered around the buggy, we witnessed a thing which we had never seen before in our family. Both father and mother were in tears. We had often seen mother in tears and father offering consolation, or father weeping and mother offering sympathy. But never before had we seen them both crying at the same time. We inquired as to the reason, and we were assured that everything was all right.

As we followed them into the house and sat down in the living room, mother told us that father had received a letter from Box "B." That was a call to go on a mission. She explained that they were happy; but they knew that it meant separation for a period of two years, and they had never been separated more than one night at a time in all of their married life.

This is only a little thing. Practically every family in the Church could tell similar and even more impressive experiences in connection with this great missionary movement. Father went, as your fathers and grandfathers went. The eighth member of our family was born after he got into the field. How I appreciate the faith of our mothers, and our grandmothers. Important has been their responsibility in missionary service.

Conference Report, April 1945, p. 108.

That Was President Smith

My soul has been subdued and my heart made tender through the passing of our great leader, President George Albert Smith. I have mingled feelings of humility, sadness, and gratitude at the passing of a prophet of God. All Israel, I am sure, has been weeping. And yet, in back of it all has been a feeling of thanksgiving for the life of this great man.

God bless the memory of President George Albert Smith. I am grateful beyond my words of expression for the close association which I have had with him in the last few years. I am grateful that my family has lived in the same ward and has come under the benign influence of his sweet spirit. I shall never cease to be grateful for the visits he made to my home while I was serving as a humble missionary in the nations of war-torn Europe at the end of World War II.

Particularly am I thankful for a visit in the still of the night when our little one lay at death's door. Without any announcement, President Smith found time to come into that home and place his hands upon the head of that little one, held in her mother's arms as she had been for many hours, and promise her complete recovery. This was President Smith; he always had time to help, particularly those who were sick and needed him most.

Conference Report, April 1951, pp. 45-46.

They Just Stood There and Visited and Visited

One of my non-Mormon friends passed away only a few days ago. He was rather prominently known, wrote for national magazines, and was chairman of the board of trustees of one of our great universities. Some months ago he came to this city to address a meeting of dairymen, most of whom were members of the Church. After the meeting was over, he came up to my home for the purpose of a visit and a renewal of friendship.

As I drove him back to the hotel that night, he turned to me, after being quiet for several moments, and said, "I don't know what it is, but each time I come among your people I experience something that I never experience anywhere else in the world. It's an intangible thing, but it's very real." He added, "I've tried to analyze it, I've tried to describe it, but the best thing I can do is to say that every time I come among your people, I get a spiritual uplift. What is it that gives me that feeling which I get nowhere else?"

Brethren and sisters, what is it? You feel it. We feel it in these great conferences of the Church. We feel it out in the stakes of Zion. We feel it in little branch meetings or in meetings with missionaries in the far parts of the earth. It's a sweet thing. It's a priceless thing. It is a mark of the divinity of this great work in which we are engaged.

I recall while living in the East some years ago, I invited one of my good friends, not a member of the Church, to attend our sacrament meeting. He promised that he would sometime. Weeks went by. I met him on the street one day following a Rotary luncheon, and he said, "I was up to your meeting last Sunday night, but you weren't there." I explained that I was visiting another ward, and then he said in answer to my inquiry as to whether he enjoyed the meeting, "Yes, I enjoyed it, especially the spirit of it, but," he said, "I wish you would tell me one thing. Why is it that when your people come to the end of a meeting and the benediction is said that they don't seem to have any place to go?" He said, "That group stood up, recognizing the meeting was over, but they just stood there and visited and visited until I thought I was never going to get out of that building. Finally, when I got into the foyer, it was more congested than ever." Well, that is a further evidence of this spirit—this spirit of love, this spirit of brotherhood that is so real, my brethren and sisters, in the Church.

Conference Report, October 1950, pp. 144-45.

Twenty-Two People Were Living in One Room

Probably the saddest part of our mission was with our refugees. These poor, unwanted souls have been driven from their once happy homes to destinations unknown. They came with all their earthly possessions on their backs, but after organizing them into branches and calling them into meetings, they sang the songs of Zion with a fervor I am sure has never been surpassed. We visited some of their homes—their shacks—where as many as twenty-two people were living in one room—four complete families! And yet they knelt together in prayer night and morning and bore testimony to us regarding the blessings of the gospel.

Now, just a word about the Welfare Program. I bring to you, my brothers and sisters, the deep gratitude and thanksgiving of the Saints in Europe. The spirit of the Welfare Program was there long before we arrived. The Saints in various countries had sent help to their less fortunate brothers and sisters in other nations. Welfare gardens had been planted. We found them among the bombed-out buildings. We ran on to many instances where following bombings, branches had joined together and pooled all their remaining supplies, food, clothing, and household articles, and turned them over to the priesthood for distribution according to need.

It was a great joy when the welfare supplies came through. It was also a great surprise to the military authorities and others to learn with what dispatch the supplies arrived from Zion after arrangements were made and the cable sent back to Zion, March 14, 1946, to start shipments. They could hardly believe that there was a church in existence with a hundred storehouses well stocked, ready to dispatch supplies to the suffering people in Europe. You have heard figures regarding the quantities that have arrived—some fifty-one carloads. That means over two hundred European carloads, or approximately two thousand tons, and I am sure that if the cost of transporting it on the European end was considered, it would total well over three quarters of a million dollars. The bulk of that, of course, has gone to the countries in greatest distress, Germany and Austria, Holland, Norway, Belgium, with quantities going to many other countries according to need.

I have faced congregations of more than a thousand Latter-day Saints where it was estimated by the mission president that more than eighty percent of the total clothing worn was clothing from Zion, sent through the Welfare Program. My brethren and sisters, do you need any further evidence of the need for this program and the inspiration back of it? I wish you could have spent a few days with me in Europe during this past year. I tell you God is directing this program. It is inspired! Had it not been so, there would have been many, many hundreds more of our Latter-day Saints perish with hunger and die of cold because of the lack of simple food commodities and clothing.

Conference Report, April 1947, pp. 155-56.

From Somewhere They Had Obtained An Old Radio

It is quite appropriate, it seems to me, that much reference has been made in this conference to conditions in Europe and the great events that have taken place there in recent months: the dedication of the temple at Bern.

Reference has been made to the European tour of the choir, the faith of the Saints, and the blessings which they enjoy today compared with only a few years ago—yes, just a short decade ago. I am very grateful to President McKay and the other members of the Presidency that Sister Benson and I were invited to attend that glorious dedication in Bern, Switzerland.

I think I have never felt in all my life the veil quite so thin as it was three weeks ago this morning as we met in the opening session of that dedication service in that lovely spot in the house of the Lord, and as we listened to the prayer offered by President McKay and the remarks which preceded that prayer.

Naturally I was deeply impressed with the contrast between conditions in Europe in 1946 when I was there last and conditions as we find them now. I have been going back in memory off and on ever since the dedication, reviewing in my mind the conditions that existed there when I went on an emergency mission in response to the First Presidency's call in 1946....

I would like to mention this morning just one simple experience to illustrate not only the changes that have come about, but also something of the influence and the power of music and the Tabernacle Choir.

We were meeting at the city of Herne with the Saints of the battered

Ruhr industrial area for their first district conference after the war. The meeting was being held in an old bombed-out schoolhouse. I do not recall exactly how many people were there, but there were several hundred. We had set the meeting for eleven o'clock in order to give them time to walk the long distances many of them had to come, some of them carrying babies in arms, because there were no public conveyances available and most of them had worn out their bicycles or were unable to get repair parts.

The district presidency had arranged, with our cooperation, a special surprise for the congregation that morning. From somewhere they had obtained an old radio which they had placed under cover in one corner of the building. At a certain moment in that service, which I shall never forget, the controls of that radio were turned to Radio Stuttgart, the American army radio station operated by a Mormon serviceman, and we heard strains of the Tabernacle Choir float out over the audience in that stirring and beautiful pioneer song, "Come, Come, Ye Saints."

After the second number, "O My Father," had been sung, I think there was not a dry eye among the adults in that audience. I saw before me an audience literally melted to tears through the singing of Mormon hymns by our great choir. It seemed as if all the cares of those suffering Saints were forgotten that morning. Even during the thirty-minute lunch period—when the most common item for lunch was a mixture of cracked grain and a little water such as we used to feed the baby chicks—even during the lunch period they talked of their blessings and expressed their gratitude for the gospel.

Then as we left that evening after the second session, the common expression was, as we bade them good-bye, "Allis gnt, Brother Benson." Well, all is good now surely. With the coming of the temples, with the material restoration that has come to those countries, and with what I hope is a deepened interest in spiritual matters—to which the temple will contribute in great measure—I hope too there will be a great increased interest in things spiritual, that those nations might be preserved in peace.

Conference Report, October 1955, pp. 106-108.

Many of These Saints Dressed in Rags

To one who has spent the major part of the last year amidst the rubble and destruction of war-torn Europe, this conference has been doubly inspirational and appreciated. As I have looked into the faces of this well-fed (almost too well-fed in many cases) audience, well-clothed, surrounded with all the comforts and blessings of life, I have found that my thoughts have many times drifted across the Atlantic to those countries, and with what I hope is a deepened interest in spiritual matters—to which the temple will contribute, brethren and sisters, as I am sure you do, many of you having descended through progenitors from those nations.

I think I shall never forget those first meetings with the Saints. They have suffered much, my brethren and sisters. We wondered just how they would receive us, what the reaction would be. Would their hearts be filled with bitterness? Would there be hatred there? Would they have soured on the Church? I well remember our first meeting at Karlsruhe. After we had made visits through Belgium, Holland, and the Scandinavian countries, we went into occupied Germany. We finally found our way to the meeting place, a partially bombed-out building located in the interior of a block. The Saints had been in session for some two hours waiting for us, hoping that we would come because the word had reached them that we might be there for the conference. And then for the first time in my life I saw almost an entire audience in tears as we walked up onto the platform, and they realized that at last, after six or seven long years, representatives from Zion, as they put it, had finally come back to them. Then as the meeting closed, prolonged at their request, they insisted we go to the door and shake hands with each one of them as they left the bombed-out building. And we noted that many of them, after they had passed through the line, went back and came through the second and third time, so happy were they to grasp our hands. As I looked into their upturned faces—pale, thin, many of these Saints dressed in rags, some of them barefooted—I could see the light of faith in their eyes as they bore testimony to the divinity of this great latter-day work and expressed their gratitude for the blessings of the Lord.

That is what a testimony does. We saw it in many countries. I say there is no greater faith, to my knowledge, anywhere in the Church than we found among those good people in Europe. Many interesting things happened as you can well imagine.

Ofttimes our meeting rooms were in almost total darkness as we were forced to close the windows, filled with cardboard instead of glass, because of a rainstorm. But the Saints insisted that we go on with the meeting. Other times we would close a meeting, and then they would ask if we could hold another before we sent them home—they were so happy to have the opportunity of meeting with us. I remember in Nuremberg that the people had waited two hours for us—we were delayed because of detours around bombed bridges and other things. Shortly after we arrived, the curfew rang. But they requested that we allow them to stay on and after the meeting was over, they were forced to stay all night in the old partially bombed-out school-house, because of curfew restrictions. Words cannot adequately express the joy of the Saints for the first mission-wide conference following the war in England, Holland, Sweden, and other countries.

We found that our members had carried on in a marvelous way. Their faith was strong, their devotion greater, and their loyalty unsurpassed. We found very little, if any, bitterness or despair. There was a spirit of fellowship and brotherhood which had extended from one mission to the other, and as we traveled, the Saints asked us to take their greetings to their brothers and sisters in other countries although their nations had been at war only a few months before. Local missionaries had carried on during the war period. In some districts there had been more baptisms than during a comparable period prior to the war.

Conference Report, April 1947, pp. 152-55.

HUGH B. BROWN

Elder Hugh B. Brown was ordained an apostle on April 10, 1958, and served as a counselor in the First Presidency to President David O. McKay from 1961 to 1970. Following President McKay's death, Elder Brown resumed his position in the Quorum of the Twelve Apostles.

He was born in Salt Lake City, Utah, October 24, 1883, to Homer Manley and Lydia J. B. Brown. The family moved to Canada fifteen years later, and much of Elder Brown's life was centered there.

On June 17, 1908, he married Zina Young Card, a daughter of Charles O. Card, the founder of Cardston, Alberta, Canada. They were married in the Salt Lake Temple and had six daughters and two sons.

Elder Brown first practiced law in Canada and later in the United States. During World War I he served overseas in the Canadian Army, attaining the rank of major. During World War II he was the Church's coordinator of LDS servicemen's activities.

He was a professor of religion and coordinator of veteran affairs at Brigham Young University from 1946 to 1950.

Elder Brown passed away in Salt Lake City on December 2, 1975.

I Went Around to the Back Door

Many things have been said about missionaries and missionary work. That has been the first public love of my life, and I have been reminded of several things that happened sixty-eight years ago when I went to England. One I should like to relate.

I had gone to a certain house several times and had been rejected and warned not to come back again, but I was prompted to go again and again. And then as I was attempting to walk past that house, I was prompted to go in and try again to make contact. I used the big brass knocker on the English door without any response. I could see a lady in the front room knitting, and I made considerable noise with that knocker. She did not come out, and I went around to the back door. There was no knocker on that door so I used my walking stick, and I knocked with considerable vigor; in fact, it echoed through all of the house.

Very soon the lady came out, and her coming out reminded me of my early days on the farm when I teased a setting hen off the nest. You know that a setting hen when she is teased off the nest comes off with her feathers going in the wrong direction, and her beak in perpetual motion, and this woman reminded me of that.

I apologized and said, "I am sorry to have interrupted you and have insisted upon an interview, but, my dear sister, I have come over six thousand miles to bring you a message which the Lord wants you to have. He sent me here to give you that message. I am going back to Canada in a few days, and I must tell you what the Lord wants you to know."

She said, "You mean the Lord sent a message to me!"

I said, "That is right; he did."

I told her of the restoration of the gospel, the organization of the Church, and the message of the restoration. She was quite impressed; and I said when I left, "I am sorry to have disturbed you, but I could not fail to carry out the message that was given to me when I came here. When we meet again, and we will meet again, you are going to say, Thank you for coming to my back door. Thank you for loving me enough to carry the message of the Lord to me. When you left I could hardly contain myself. I was worried, disturbed, and wondered what it was all about. I finally went to the mission home, got some literature, studied, and became a member of the Church with my family.'"

Ten years later I was in England again, this time as a soldier, and at the end of the meeting a lady came up with two grown daughters. She said, "I do thank God and thank you that you came to my door with that message many years ago. I and my daughters joined the Church and we are going to Utah in a short time, and we thank God that you had the courage, the fortitude, and the faith to come to me with that divine message and to leave it with me in the name of the Lord."

My brethren and sisters, I want to bear witness to you as to the divinity of this work. From the center of my heart to the ends of my fingers and toes, I know that this is the work of God. I know that the gospel has been restored. I know that the men who are leading the Church are inspired and directed by him who appointed them. I know that the gospel will roll forth until it fills the whole earth, and I am looking forward to the time when all of us will be united on the other side and carry on the great work that we have so falteringly tried to do here on earth.

I leave this testimony with you, and my blessing.

Hugh B. Brown, "A Missionary and His Message," *Ensign*, July 1972, p. 86.

When the Bell Rings

Let me tell a story to illustrate the point that a man must respond to his better self if he is going to be a worthy holder of the priesthood.

The story is told that the Arabians, when they are training their horses, put them to a final test of character and stamina. It is said that the finest of the Arabian horses which are kept for breeding stock are trained from the time they are colts to respond to a bell which rings intermittently at the tent of the master. Wherever they are and whatever they are doing, they must run to the tent of the master when the bell rings. Their mothers were taught it before them, and they respond, and the colts, running beside the mother, habitually as time goes on respond to the bell and know that it is the call of duty.

When the colts are three years old, they are placed in a pole corral that they can see through. They are left there three days and nights without food or water. At the end of the third day hay and grain and water are placed just outside the corral.

You can imagine the eagerness of the young colts as they look through the bars at the food and water. When the gate is opened the young colts rush out, and just as they are about to reach the food and water, the bell rings. Only those of them that have stamina enough to respond to the bell and resist the urge of appetite are kept for the breeding stock of the future.

Brethren, as we go forward, we become increasingly aware of the fact that there is a bell which rings very frequently throughout life. Sometimes men become unresponsive or hard of hearing and disregard the bell to their own sorrow. You young men are going to hear it many times between now and the time you are our age. We plead with you to resist the call of appetite and passion and hearken to the bell which is your conscience. If you are tempted to do wrong, there will always be something within you saying, "Don't do it."

Hearken and respond to that bell, and you will be worthy of the confidence that the President of the Church has in you, worthy to take over the responsibilities now held by your fathers, your brothers, your leaders.

Conference Report, April 1963, p. 91.

Would Anyone Like to Undertake Such a Task?

I believe Joseph Smith was a prophet because he did many superhuman things. One was translating the Book of Mormon, which is a history of the ancient inhabitants of America. Some people will not agree, but I submit that Joseph Smith in translating the Book of Mormon did a super-human work. I ask anyone to undertake to write the story of the ancient inhabitants of America, to write as he did without any source material.

He must include in the story fifty-four chapters dealing with wars, twenty-one historical chapters, fifty-five chapters on visions and prophecies (and remember, when the writer begins to write on visions and prophecies, he must have the record agree meticulously with the Bible). He must write seventy-one chapters on doctrine and exhortation, and here too, he must check every statement with the scriptures or he will be proved to be a fraud. He must write twenty-one chapters on the ministry of Christ, and everything the writer claims Jesus said and did and every testimony he writes in the book about him must agree absolutely with the New Testament.

Would anyone like to undertake such a task? I point out, too, that he must employ figures of speech, similes, metaphors, narration, exposition, description, oratory, epic, lyric, logic, and parables. I ask the writer to remember that the man who translated the Book of Mormon was a young man who had very little schooling, and yet he dictated that book in just a little over two months and made very few, if any, corrections.

For over one hundred years, some of the best students and scholars of the world have been trying to prove from the Bible that the Book of Mormon is a fraud, but not one of them has been able to prove that anything in it is contrary to the scriptures, the Bible, the word of God.

Conference Report, October 1967, pp. 119-20.

Send Us Water

Some may feel that in some far-off part of the Church there is not much hope. Sometimes we say, "Well, if you could send us a General Authority more often, we would be more inspired." The Church is getting too big, as Brother Lee has explained, for the General Authorities to attend all of the conferences.

I am reminded of what happened to a captain of a ship down in the South Atlantic. He had run out of fresh water. His crew were athirst. Another ship hove in sight, and he signaled, "Send us water" and the signal come back, "Let down your buckets, there is fresh water all around you. You are in the Gulf Stream." They let down their buckets and found it was true. They had not realized that the course of the Gulf Stream, driven out into the briny deep, had maintained its virtues, so to speak. They were able to save themselves by that which was all around them, yet they did not know it.

Brethren, there is available to you, wherever you are, the blessings, the opportunities, the privileges of teaching the gospel of Christ, if you will let down your bucket into the gulf stream of the Holy Spirit, which is everywhere.

Conference Report, October 1963, p. 85.

You Will Be Honorable

First, I think I would like to say to the young men who are listening and who are present that I wish you would cultivate a sense of humor.

In the army while in the first world war, one of our boys who was a pretty good fighter was challenged in England to a fight. This young man, our Mormon boy, had the habit of smiling all the way through a fight. One of the men whom he was pitted against was champion, and during the fight he said to his attendants between rounds, "I can't lick that guy unless I can knock that grin off his face." He was not able to do it. That smile represented a courage of cold steel, and the Mormon boy won the battle.

Now as to the story: In 1906 the government of Canada passed a law that was known as the Militia Act, comparable to the home guard here. They sent out into all the provinces a call for men to take training preparatory to what Lord Roberts said was sure to come, a world war. A young man was sent to Cardston to recruit some of our men. This young fellow was the son of a prominent military man. He had been raised with a silver spoon in his mouth, evidently. He was one of those fellows who had a jaunty moustache and a little swagger stick, and he wore a monocle, a one-eye glass. He was a most objectionable fellow in the eyes of our young men. In fact, his monocle reminds me of another story.

I was standing one day between Piccadilly Circus and Leicester Square talking to an American officer during the first world war. We saw a man coming down the sidewalk with his hat on one side, swinging a swagger stick, a Charlie Chaplin moustache, and a monocle. I said to the officer, "I wonder why those fellows wear a one-eye glass instead of two."

"Well," he said, "I'll tell you. A guy like that can see more with one eye than he can comprehend."

Well, such was the man who came out to recruit the Mormon boys. He spent two weeks in Cardston. He was sent out to organize a squadron of mounted men. He did not get one recruit during that two weeks. A lot of them came in and responded to his call, but did not sign up. He went back to Ottawa and reported the Mormons were disloyal and ought to be expelled from Canada.

The member of parliament from our district at that time was W. A. Buchanan, who knew our people very well. The matter was taken to the floor of the parliament, and considerable agitation was whipped up. Mr.

Buchanan arose and said, "If you will allow some of their own men to become officers, you will get all the Mormon boys you want."

The government finally accepted his recommendation, and they sent word out to President Edward J. Wood to appoint some men to go and take training, which he did. I happened to be one who was called in by President Wood and called on a three-year mission, to go to Calgary and take training as a militia officer.

While I was in training, a young Mormon boy came into the camp. He was awkward. He was not educated very well, but he was a young Mormon boy who had been taught to live the gospel. After one parade, when he had gone through everything backwards, he was called by the captain to come into his office. The captain said, "I have noticed you, young fellow. You are from Cardston, aren't you?"

He said, "Yes, sir."

"You are a Mormon, I suppose."

"Yes, sir."

"Well, I just wanted to make friends with you. Will you have a glass of beer?"

"Sir, I do not drink liquor."

The captain said, "The @%#$& you don't. Maybe you will have a cigar then."

He said, "Thank you, sir, but I do not smoke."

The captain seemed much annoyed by this, and he dismissed the boy from the room.

When the young man went back to his quarters, some of the lesser officers accosted him angrily and said, "You fool, don't you realize the captain was trying to make a friend of you, and you insulted him to his face?"

The young Mormon boy answered, "Gentlemen, if I must be untrue to my ideals and my people and do things that I have been instructed all my life I should not do, I'll quit the army."

When the time came for the final examination in that camp, the captain sent this young man down to Calgary from Sarcee Camp to do some work for him, and they were having examinations while he was gone. When he returned the captain said, "Now you go in the other room there, and I will give you the list of questions, and you can write your examination."

He went in and returned and said, "Sir, all the books we have studied are there on that desk. Surely you don't want me to write my examination there where I can turn to those books."

The captain said, "That is just what I do want. I know from my knowledge of you that you will not open a one of those books. You will be honorable, you will be honest, and I trust you."

Well, that young man, while overseas later on in the war, was sent for by his captain, who had become a lieutenant colonel, in response to a call from general headquarters for the best man he had in his battalion. They had a special mission for him to perform. They said, "We don't care anything about his education or his training. We want a man who can't be broken when put under test. We want a man of character." The lieutenant colonel, his former captain, selected and assigned this young man who had the courage to stand before him and say, "I do not smoke. I do not drink."

I cite that as a type of thing that happens sometimes in military life.

Well, at the end of the training period we organized a squadron and took them to Calgary in the years 1912-14, when, as you know, the first world war broke out, Canada and England having been in the war for some years before the United States came in. Our Mormon boys made a great name for themselves, both in Canada and overseas.

Conference Report, April 1969, pp. 111-13.

Examination for Discovery

I should like to give some reasons for this faith and attempt to justify my allegiance to the Church. Perhaps I can do this best by referring again to an interview I had in London, England, in 1939, just before the outbreak of World War II.

I had met a very prominent English gentleman, a member of the House of Commons and formerly one of the justices of the supreme court of Britain. In a series of conversations on various subjects, "vexations of the soul," he called them, we talked about business and law; about politics, international relations, and war; and we frequently discussed religion.

He called me on the phone one day and asked if I would meet him at his office and explain some phases of my faith. He said, "There is going to be a war, and you will have to return to America, and we may not meet again." His statement regarding the imminence of war and the possibility that we would not meet again proved to be prophetic.

When I went to his office, he said he had been intrigued by some things I had told about my church. He asked me if I would prepare a brief on Mormonism and discuss it with him as I would discuss a legal problem. He said, "You have told me that you believe that Joseph Smith was a prophet and that you believe that God the Father and Jesus of Nazareth appeared to him in vision."

"I cannot understand," he said, "how a barrister and solicitor from Canada, a man trained in logic and evidence and unemotional cold fact, could accept such absurd statements. What you tell me about Joseph Smith seems fantastic, but I wish you would take three days at least to prepare a brief and permit me to examine it and question you on it."

I suggested that, as I had been working on such a brief for more than fifty years, we proceed at once to have an examination for discovery, which is briefly a meeting of the opposing sides in a lawsuit where the plaintiff and defendant, with their attorneys, meet to examine each other's claims and see whether they can find some area of agreement and thus save the time of the court later on.

I said perhaps we could find some common ground from which we could discuss my "fantastic ideas." He agreed, and we proceeded with our "examination for discovery."

Because of time limitations, I can only give a condensed or abbreviated synopsis of the three-hour conversation that followed. I began by asking, "May I proceed, sir, on the assumption that you are a Christian?"

"I am."

"I assume that you believe in the Bible—the Old and New Testaments?"

"I do!"

"Do you believe in prayer?"

"I do!"

"You say that my belief that God spoke to a man in this age is fantastic and absurd?"

"To me it is."

"Do you believe that God ever did speak to anyone?"

"Certainly, all through the Bible we have evidence of that."

"Did he speak to Adam?"

"Yes."

"To Enoch, Noah, Abraham, Moses, Jacob, and to others of the prophets?"

"I believe he spoke to each of them."

"Do you believe that contact between God and man ceased when Jesus appeared on the earth?"

"Certainly not. Such communication reached its climax, its apex at that time."

"Do you believe that Jesus of Nazareth was the Son of God?"

"He was."

"Do you believe, sir, that after the resurrection of Christ, God ever spoke to any man?"

He thought for a moment and then said, "I remember one Saul of Tarsus who was going down to Damascus to persecute the saints and who had a vision, was stricken blind, in fact, and heard a voice."

"Whose voice did he hear?"

"Well," he said, "the voice said 'I am Jesus whom thou persecutest: it is hard for thee to kick against the pricks.'"

"Do you believe that actually took place?"

"I do."

"Then, my Lord"—that is the way we address judges in the British commonwealth—"my Lord, I am submitting to you in all seriousness that it was standard procedure in Bible times for God to talk to men."

"I think I will admit that, but it stopped shortly after the first century of the Christian era."

"Why do you think it stopped?"

"I can't say."

"You think that God hasn't spoken since then?"

"Not to my knowledge."

"May I suggest some possible reasons why he has not spoken. Perhaps it is because he cannot. He has lost the power."

He said, "Of course, that would be blasphemous."

"Well, then, if you don't accept that, perhaps he doesn't speak to men because he doesn't love us anymore. He is no longer interested in the affairs of men."

"No," he said, "God loves all man, and he is no respecter of persons."

"Well, then, if you don't accept that he doesn't love us, then the only other possible answer as I see it is that we don't need him. We have made such rapid strides in education and science that we don't need God anymore."

And then he said, and his voice trembled as he thought of impending war, "Mr. Brown, there never was a time in the history of the world when the voice of God was needed as it is needed now. Perhaps you can tell me why he doesn't speak."

My answer was, "He does speak, he has spoken; but men need faith to hear him."

Conference Report, September 1967, pp. 117-18.

No, I'm Not in Trouble

And here I should like to introduce a story coming out of the first world war. I had a companion, a fellow officer, who was a very rich man, highly educated. A lawyer, he was powerful and self-sufficient, and he said to me as we often talked of religion (because he knew who I was), "There is nothing in life that I would like to have that I cannot buy with my money."

Shortly thereafter he and I with two other officers were assigned to go to the city of Arras, France, which was under siege. It had been evacuated, and upon arrival there we thought there was no one in the city. We noted that the fire of the enemy was concentrated on the cathedral. We made our way to that cathedral and went in. There we found a little woman kneeling at an altar. We paused, respecting her devotion. Then shortly she arose, wrapped her little shawl around her frail shoulders, and came tottering down the aisle. The man among us who could speak better French said, "Are you in trouble?"

She straightened her shoulders, pulled in her chin, and said, "No, I'm not in trouble. I was in trouble when I came here, but I've left it there at the altar."

"And what was your trouble?"

She said, "I received word this morning that my fifth son has given his life for France. Their father went first, and then one by one all of them have gone. But," straightening again, "I have no trouble; I've left it there because I believe in the immortality of the soul. I believe that men will live after death. I know that I shall meet my loved ones again."

When the little soul went out, there were tears in the eyes of the men who were there, and the one who had said to me that he could purchase anything with money turned to me and said, "You and I have seen men in battle display courage and valor that is admirable, but in all my life I have never seen anything to compare with the faith, the fortitude, and the courage of that little woman."

Then he said, "I would give all the money I have if I could have something of what she has."

Conference Report, October 1969, pp. 106-107.

Father, Are You There?

I think one of the first things that every young person should do is attempt to get acquainted with God. I mean that in a very literal sense. I mean it in the sense that we are able to go to him and obtain the kind of help that we need. I remember when I was quite a lad (and that's remembering a long way back). I remember my mother said to me when I went to go on my mission in 1904 (and that's before some of you were born).

She said, "My boy, you are going a long ways away from me now. Do you remember that when you were a little lad you used to have bad dreams and get frightened? Your bedroom was just off mine, and frequently you would cry out in the night and say, 'Mother, are you there?' And I would answer 'Yes, my boy, I'm here. Everything is all right. Turn over and go to sleep.' You always did. Knowing that I was there gave you courage."

"Now," she said, "you will be about 6,000 miles away, and though you may cry out for me I cannot answer you."

She added this: "There is one who can, and if you call to him, he'll hear you when you call. He will respond to your appeal. You just say, 'Father, are you there?' and there will come into your heart the comfort and solace such as you knew as a boy when I answered you."

I want to say to you young people that many times since then in many and varying conditions I have cried out, "Father, are you there?" I made that plea when in the mission field we were mobbed almost every night, driven from place to place. We were beaten, expelled from cities, our lives threatened. Every time before I went out to those meetings I would say, "Father, are you there?" And though I didn't hear a voice and I didn't see his person, I want to tell you young people he replied to me with the comfort and assurance and testimony of his presence. It made me unafraid; and with that presence, I am grateful to say, we did not suffer much.

> BYU Stakes Fireside Address, "Father, Are You There?" October 8, 1967 [Provo, Utah: Brigham Young University Press], pp. 5-6.

I Only Touched Ground Once

I would like to call your attention to what happens to a man in this church when he is converted to the truth. I hope you are all converts. I was in a meeting not long ago and I asked how many were converts. Probably fifty per cent raised their hands. I said, "I advise the rest of you to get converted." You need to be converts. I would like to say this in passing, that in the years that have passed, and they are many, I have continued to be a convert to The Church of Jesus Christ of Latter-day Saints; and for that I thank God. He has been good to me in that he has headed me off when I would have gone my own way. He has known better than I do what was good for me, and he has been willing and gracious to make provision for the things that he could see and I couldn't see would happen to me, unless he took a part; and he took it. For this I am extremely grateful.

I said I have had contact with him. In 1904 I went to England on a mission. President Grant sent me down to Norwich. When I got into Norwich the president of the district sent me down to Cambridge. He said, "I want you to go with Elder Downs (he was a man 45 years old and I was 21). Elder Downs will leave the morning after you get there for France, because his mission is completed. There is not another Latter-day Saint within 120 miles of Cambridge, so you will be alone."

He said, "You might be interested to know, Brother Brown, that the last Mormon elder that was in Cambridge was driven out by a mob at the point of a gun and was told the next Mormon elder that stepped inside the city limits would be shot on sight." He said, "I thought you would be glad to know that."

I wasn't glad to know it, but I thought it was well that I did know it.

We went to Cambridge. There were great signs all over the city that they had heard we were coming. They had signs indicating their antipathy. That was their method of welcoming us. One big sign at the railway station was of a large man with a long beard, with a woman lying at his feet with her head on a block. Underneath it said, "Will you go into polygamy or won't you?" That was the reception we received.

Elder Downs left the next morning after telling me how to prepare my tracts, and I went out on Friday morning and tracted all morning without any response except a slammed door in my face. I tracted all afternoon with the same response, and I came home pretty well discouraged. But I decided to tract Saturday morning, although it wasn't required. I went out and tracted all morning and got the same results. I came home dejected and downhearted, and I thought I ought to go home. I thought the Lord had made a mistake in sending me to Cambridge.

I was sitting by that little alleged fire they have in England, with a big granddaddy clock at the side of the so-called fire. I was feeling sorry for myself, and I heard a knock at the front door. The lady of the house answered the door. I heard a voice say, "Is there an Elder Brown lives here?" I thought, "Oh, oh, here it is!"

She said, "Why, yes, he's in the front room. Come in, please."

He came in and said, "Are you Elder Brown?"

I was not surprised that he was surprised. I said, "Yes, sir."

He said, "Did you leave this tract at my door?"

Well, my name and address were on it. Though I was attempting at that time to get ready to practice law, I didn't know how to answer it. I said, "Yes, sir, I did."

He said, "Last Sunday there were seventeen of us heads of families left the Church of England. We went to my home where I have a rather large room. Each of us has a large family, and we filled the large room with men, women and children. We decided that we would pray all through the week that the Lord would send us a new pastor. When I came home tonight I was discouraged; I thought our prayer had not been answered. But when I found this tract under my door, I knew the Lord had answered our prayer. Will you come tomorrow night and be our new pastor?"

Now, I hadn't been in the mission field three days. I didn't know anything about missionary work, and he wanted me to be their pastor. But I was reckless enough to say, "Yes, I'll come." And I repented from then until the time of the meeting.

He left, and took my appetite with him! I called in the lady of the house and told her I didn't want any tea. I went up to my room and prepared for bed. I knelt at my bed. My young brothers and sisters, for the first time in my life I talked with God. I told him of my predicament. I pleaded for his help. I asked him to guide me. I pleaded that he would take it off my hands. I got up and went to bed and couldn't sleep and got out and prayed again, and kept that up all night—but I really talked with God.

The next morning I told the landlady I didn't want any breakfast, and I went up on the campus in Cambridge and walked all morning. I came in at noon and told her I didn't want any lunch. Then I walked all afternoon. I had a short-circuited mind—all that I could think of was that I have got to go down there tonight and be a pastor.

I came back to my room at 6:00 and I sat there meditating, worrying, wondering. (Let me in parenthesis tell you that since that time I have had the experience of sitting beside a man who was condemned to die the next morning. As I sat and watched his emotions I was reminded of how I felt that night. I think I felt just as bad as he did.) The execution time was drawing near. Finally the clock said 6:45. I got up and put on my long Prince Albert coat, my stiff hat which I had acquired in Norwich, took my walking cane (which we always carried in those days), my kid gloves, put a Bible under my arm, and dragged myself down to that building, literally. I just made one track all the way.

Just as I got to the gate the man came out, the man I had seen the night before. He bowed very politely and said, "Come in, Reverend, sir." I had never been called that before. I went in and saw the room filled with people, and they all stood up to honor their new pastor, and that scared me to death.

Then I had come to the point where I began to think what I had to do, and I realized I had to say something about singing. I suggested that we sing "O My Father." I was met with a blank stare. We sang it—it was a terrible cowboy solo. Then I thought, if I could get these people to turn around and kneel by their chairs, they wouldn't be looking at me while I prayed. I asked them if they would and they responded readily. They all knelt down, and I knelt down, and for the second time in my life I talked with God. All fear left me. I didn't worry any more. I was turning it over to him.

I said to him, among other things, "Father in Heaven, these folks have left the Church of England. They have come here tonight to hear the truth. You know that I am not prepared to give them what they want, but Thou art, O God, the one that can; and if I can be an instrument through whom

You speak, very well, but please take over."

When we arose most of them were weeping, as was I.

Wisely I dispensed with the second hymn, and I started to talk. I talked forty-five minutes. I don't know what I said. I didn't talk—God spoke through me, as subsequent events proved. And he spoke so powerfully to that group that at the close of that meeting they came and put their arms around me, held my hands. They said, "This is what we have been waiting for. Thank God you came."

I told you I dragged myself down to that meeting. On my way back home that night I only touched ground once, I was so elated that God had taken off my hands an insuperable task for man.

Within three months every man, woman and child in that audience was baptized a member of the Church. I didn't baptize them because I was transferred. But they all joined the Church and most of them came to Utah and Idaho. I have seen some of them in recent years. They are elderly people now, but they say they never have attended such a meeting, a meeting where God spoke to them.

BYU Stakes Fireside Address, "Father, Are You There?" October 8, 1967, pp. 12-15.

Thank You, God

While I was acting as servicemen's coordinator, I was in London, England. I sent the following telegram to the senior chaplain of a large camp near Liverpool: "I'll be in your camp tomorrow morning at 10:00. Kindly notify all Mormon boys in your camp that we'll hold a meeting."

When I arrived the next morning I met seventy-five young men, all in uniform. They were delighted to see me, although I knew none of them. They were glad to see someone from home.

There stepped out from the crowd a man who, after shaking hands, said, "I'm the one to whom you sent your telegram. I'm the chaplain of this camp. I didn't get your telegram until this morning (that is, Sunday morning). Upon receipt of it, I made a careful inquiry. I found there were 76 Mormon boys in this camp, and 75 of them are here. One is in the hospital."

He said, "I wish you'd tell me, Mr. Brown, how you do it. I have six hundred men in my church in this camp, and if I gave them six months notice they couldn't meet that record. Tell me how you do it."

"Well," I said, "if you come into our meeting we'll show you how we do it." And so he accompanied me into the hut, and before us sat these seventy five young men. I had the minister sit next to me.

I said, "How many of you fellows have been on missions?" Fully fifty percent of them raised their hands. I pointed to six of them and said, "Come here and administer the sacrament." I pointed to six others and said, "Come here and be prepared to speak." I looked at my friend, the minister, and he had his mouth open. He had never seen such a thing.

And then I said, "Fellows, what shall we sing this morning?" And with one voice they said, "Come, Come, Ye Saints!" And I said, "Who can lead the music?" and most of them raised their hands. I selected one. "Who can play this portable organ?" And again there was a fine showing, and one was selected.

Now, we didn't have any books, but the man at the organ sounded a chord, and those young men stood, shoulders back and chins pulled in, and they sang all the verses of "Come, Come, Ye Saints." Now, I have heard that sung all over the Church many times, even by the Tabernacle Choir, to whom I apologize for what I am going to say. I have never heard "Come, Come, Ye Saints" sung with such fervor, such conviction, such power as those young men sang it. When they came to that last verse: "And should we die before our journey's through, happy day, all is well," I tell you it was thrilling. And as I looked at my friend again I found him weeping.

After the prayer, one of the boys knelt at the sacrament table, and he said, "Oh God, the Eternal Father..." and then he paused for what seemed to be a full minute before proceeding. At the close of the meeting, I went and looked him up. I put my arm across his shoulder and said, "What's the matter, lad?"

He said, "Why?"

"Well you seemed to have difficulty in asking a blessing on the bread. Has something happened?"

"Well sir," he said, "a few hours ago I was over Germany and France on a bombing mission. We had made our run, left our calling cards (meaning the bombs), and when we gained altitude and were about to return across the channel, we ran into heavy flak. My tail assembly was pretty well shot away, one of my engines was out, a number of my crew were wounded, and it looked like a hopeless situation. It seemed like no power in heaven or earth could get us back across the Channel to a landing field. But," he said, "Brother Brown, up there I remembered what my mother had said to me. (And this I want to say to this vast audience, both those that are here and those that are listening in.) This is what my mother said: 'If ever you find yourself in a situation where man can't help you, call on God.' I had been told that same thing in Primary, in the seminaries, in Sunday School: 'If ever you need help and man can't help you, call on God.' Although it seemed hopeless and impossible, I said, 'Oh God, the Eternal Father, please sustain this ship until we get back into England.' . . . Brother Brown, he did just that.

"When I heard of this meeting I ran all the way to get here, and when I knelt at the table and named his name again, I remembered shamefully that I had not stopped to say, 'thank you.' And that's the reason I paused, to express my gratitude for the goodness of God."

Well, we went on with our meeting and these young men spoke, and they spoke with power and conviction. Every one who heard them was thrilled by the evidence of their faith, and my friend, the chaplain, continued to weep. When they had finished talking, I said, "Fellows, we'll have to dismiss." (That meeting was not like this; it had to be dismissed on time.) I said, "We'll have to dismiss or you won't get any chow."

They said, "We can have chow any time. Let's have a testimony meeting."

"Why," I said, "if you have a testimony meeting you'll be here another two hours."

They repeated with one voice, "Please let us have a testimony meeting."

I turned to my friend, the minister, and said, "Now I know this is unusual for you. We've been here two hours and we're going to be here another two hours. We'll excuse you if you prefer to withdraw."

He put his hand on my knee and said, "Please, Sir, may I remain?" And, of course, I encouraged him to stay, and then for two solid hours those young men, one after another, stood up and bore witness of the truth of the gospel. My only job was to say, "You're next, and then you, and then you," because all of them wanted to get up at once. It was a glorious occasion.

Finally there came an end. We dismissed, and this minister turned to me and said, "Mr. Brown, I have been a minister of the gospel for 21 years but this has been the greatest spiritual experience of my life." And again he said, "How do you do it? How did you know which of those fellows to call on?"

I replied, "It didn't make any difference which one I called on. They are all prepared. And this could happen in any camp anywhere in the world where there are seventy-five young Mormon boys."

I relate this to you, my dear students, that you may realize the value of participation—the value of a conviction of the truth—and that you may take advantage of every opportunity to bear witness to that truth.

"An Eternal Quest—Freedom Of The Mind," an address given to the BYU Student Body, May 13, 1969.

The Gardener and the Currant Bush

In the early dawn, a young gardener was pruning his trees and shrubs. He had one choice currant bush which had gone too much to wood. He feared therefore that it would produce little, if any, fruit.

Accordingly, he trimmed and pruned the bush and cut it back. In fact, when he had finished, there was little left but stumps and roots.

Tenderly he considered what was left. It looked so sad and deeply hurt. On every stump there seemed to be a tear where the pruning knife had cut away the growth of early spring. The poor bush seemed to speak to him, and he thought he heard it say, "Oh, how could you be so cruel to me; you who claim to be my friend, who planted me and cared for me when I was young, and nurtured and encouraged me to grow? Could you not see that I was rapidly responding to your care? I was nearly half as large as the trees across the fence, and might soon have become like one of them. But now you've cut my branches back; the green, attractive leaves are gone, and I am in disgrace among my fellows."

The young gardener looked at the weeping bush and heard its plea with sympathetic understanding. His voice was full of kindness as he said, "Do not cry; what I have done to you was necessary that you might be a prize currant bush in my garden. You were not intended to give shade or shelter by your branches. My purpose when I planted you was that you should bear fruit. When I want currants, a tree, regardless of its size, cannot supply the need.

"No, my little currant bush, if I had allowed you to continue to grow as you had started, all your strength would have gone to wood; your roots would not have gained a firm hold, and the purpose for which I brought you into my garden would have been defeated. Your place would have been taken by another, for you would have been barren. You must not weep; all this will be for your good; and some day, when you see more clearly, when you are richly laden with luscious fruit, you will thank me and say, 'Surely, he was a wise and loving gardener. He knew the purpose of my being, and I thank him now for what I then thought was cruelty.'"

Some years later, this young gardener was in a foreign land, and he himself was growing. He was proud of his position and ambitious for the future.

One day an unexpected vacancy entitled him to promotion. The goal to which he had aspired was now almost within his grasp, and he was proud of the rapid growth which he was making.

But for some reason unknown to him, another was appointed in his stead, and he was asked to take another relatively unimportant post, one which, under the circumstances, caused his friends to feel that he had failed.

The young man staggered to his tent and knelt beside his cot and wept. He knew now that he could never hope to have what he had thought so desirable. He cried to God and said, "Oh, how could you be so cruel to me? You who claim to be my friend—you who brought me here and nurtured and encouraged me to grow. Could you not see that I was almost equal to the other men whom I have so long admired? But now I have been cut down. I am in disgrace among my fellows. Oh, how could you do this to me?"

He was humiliated and chagrined, and a drop of bitterness was in his heart, when he seemed to hear an echo from the past. Where had he heard those words before? They seemed familiar.

Memory whispered: "I'm the gardener here."

He caught his breath. Ah, that was it—the currant bush! But why should that long-forgotten incident come to him in the midst of his hour of tragedy? And memory answered with words which he himself had spoken: "Do not cry . . . what I have done to you was necessary . . . you were not intended for what you sought to be, . . . if I had allowed you to continue . . . you would have failed in the purpose for which I planted you and my plans for you would have been defeated. You must not weep; some day when you are richly laden with experience you will say, 'He was a wise gardener. He knew the purpose of my earth life. I thank him now for what I thought was cruel.'"

His own words were the medium by which his prayer was answered. There was no bitterness in his heart as he humbly spoke again to God and said, "I know you now. You are the gardener, and I the currant bush. Help me, dear God, to endure the pruning, and to grow as you would have me grow; to take my allotted place in life and ever more to say, 'Thy will not mine be done.'"

Another lapse of time in our story. Forty years have passed. The former gardener and officer sits by his fireside with wife and children and grandchildren. He tells them the story of the currant bush—his own story; and as he kneels in prayer with them, he reverently says to God, "Help us all to understand the purpose of our being, and be ever willing to submit to thy will and not insist upon our own. We remember that in another garden called Gethsemane the choicest of all thy sons was glorified by submission unto thy will."

As they arose from prayer, this family group, they joined in singing a familiar hymn which now had for them new meaning.

"It may not be on the mountain height,
Or over the stol—my sea;
It may not be at the battle's front
My Lord will have need of me.

So trusting my all to thy tender care,
And knowing thou lovest me,
I'll do thy will with a heart sincere;
I'll be what you want me to be."

The father closed home evening with the lines:

"My will—not thine be done," turned paradise into a desert.

"Thy will not mine," turned the desert into a paradise, and made Gethsemane the gate of heaven.

Brown, Hugh B., *Eternal Quest*, [Salt Lake City: Bookcraft, 1956], pp. 243-46.

THEODORE M. BURTON

Elder Theodore M. Burton was born in Salt Lake City March 27, 1907, to Theodore Taylor and Florence Moyle Burton. He earned B.A. and M.A. degrees at the University of Utah and in 1951 obtained his doctorate at Purdue University.

Elder Burton has spent much of his life in Europe in Church and government service. He served as a missionary in the Swiss-German Mission from 1927 to 1930. In 1957 he returned to Europe to preside over the Church's West German Mission for three years, and then from 1962 to 1964 he served as president of the European Mission.

Serving at his side in these assignments was his wife, Minnie Susan Preece, whom he married in the Salt Lake Temple February 23, 1933. They have one son, Robert Preece Burton.

In 1964, Elder Burton was appointed managing director of the priesthood genealogy program of the Church. In 1972 he was appointed president of the Genealogical Society.

Elder Burton was sustained to the First Quorum of the Seventy on October 1, 1976. He passed away in Salt Lake City on December 22, 1989.

There's an Eagle in Your Chicken Yard

I visited 1,710 missionaries, and I am proud of them and their spirit of devotion. There is a good spirit among them, and they have an esprit de corps which is uniting them in spirit. They are catching the great vision of the work which they have to do. They are beginning to realize now who they are.

This concept of knowing who you are is a very important concept, and I would just like to tell you a little story that was told to me by John Bennion, one of my missionaries, which I think illustrates this principle very well. It is a story about a salesman who came into a rather isolated valley on a selling campaign. He had some selling to do, and as he looked around for a place to stay that night, he found no hotel, no rooming house, no boardinghouse, no place where he could stay. So he did what all good salesmen do when caught in a predicament of this kind. He looked around for the finest house he could see in this valley, went up, and knocked on the door. When a man came to the door, he introduced himself and said, "I am sorry to bother you, but I am looking for a place to stay tonight, and I can find neither hotel nor rooms available. Would it be possible for you to put me up tonight?"

The man opened the door in true western hospitality and said, "Stranger, come on in and make yourself at home."

So the man came in and made himself at home, and they had a very pleasant evening together—such a very pleasant evening that in the morning, he decided he would get up and help his newfound friend with his chores. He took up a bucket of grain and went out to the back of the house to the chicken yard to feed the chickens. As he started to feed the chickens, all of a sudden he called excitedly to the man, "Hey, mister, come quick. There's an eagle in your chicken yard."

"Oh," the rancher said, "don't worry about that."

He said, "You don't understand. That's a vicious bird. If you don't get him out of your chicken yard, he'll kill all your chickens!"

"Oh," the rancher said, "don't worry about it."

"But that's a golden eagle!" he cried.

Then the rancher said, "Let me tell you the story, and then you'll understand. Last year some of my boys went with me up into the mountains, and there on a cliff below us we found an eagle's nest. In that eagle's nest were three eggs, and so we let one of the boys down the cliff with a rope, and he picked up two of those eggs from the eagle's nest and brought them back up with him. When we got home, we put them under a brooding hen. One of those eggs hatched out. That's that eagle. You see, that mother hen was his mother, and all the rest of those chickens are his brothers and sisters. That's no eagle. That's a chicken."

The salesman looked over into the chicken yard and sure enough, there was the eagle scratching around in the chicken yard with all of the rest of the chickens and picking up grains of corn just as a chicken would. Then he said to the rancher, "Do you mind if I perform an experiment on that bird?"

The rancher said, "Go ahead, he can't lay any eggs."

So he walked over and picked up that eagle in his hand, looked him right in the eye, and said, "Thou art an eagle. Take to thy wings and fly!"

But the eagle just blinked at him with those big yellow eagle eyes, ruffled up his feathers, and turned his head sideways and looked him up and down. Then he hopped down to the ground and started to scratch in the dirt after grains of corn.

The rancher laughed at the salesman and said, "See, I told you he was just a chicken."

The salesman shook his head and he said, "It just isn't right." Then he went out on his selling campaign, but did not finish, so he returned that night and said, "I am sorry to bother you again, but could I stay another night?"

The rancher said, "Look, you stay just as long as you have a mind to. You will always be welcome here."

So he spent another very pleasant evening and the next morning got up, picked up his bucket of grain, and went out to feed those chickens again. After he had fed the chickens he looked at that eagle. He went over and picked him up, raised him on his hand, and looked him right in the eye and said, "Thou art an eagle. Take to thy wings and fly!" But the eagle just blinked at him with those big yellow eagle eyes, ruffled up his feathers, cocked his head, and looked him up and down, then hopped to the ground and started to scratch for grains of corn again.

The rancher laughed again and said, "It's hopeless. Give it up." Well, the salesman went out to sell another day, but he still did not finish, so he stayed a third night, and that third morning he went out to feed those chickens again. He fed them and then looked at that eagle. It was very early in the morning, and the sun was just coming up over the mountain as he reached down and lifted up that eagle and turned him this time so that he had to look right at the sun. Then he said, "Thou art a golden eagle. Take to thy wings and fly!"

But the eagle just blinked at him with those big yellow eagle eyes, ruffled up his feathers, cocked his head, and looked at him again. But as he did so, the sun got in his eyes, so he raised his head to look at the sun, and all of a sudden he began to tremble. Then he spread those great wings and off he flew, and that was the last that was ever seen of that eagle.

Now, he was no longer a chicken. He was an eagle, the king of the air, in the element where he belonged. He was free. A golden eagle, the king of the birds!

I am convinced that there are too many golden eagles among us who are convinced that we are chickens. This is no time for us ever to be chickens. This is a time for us as well as a time for our missionaries to realize who we are.

Conference Report, April 1962, pp. 55-57.

We Have Enough—Don't Bring Any More

In February of this year we had a terrible storm which crashed down upon Northern Europe. The wind blowing in from the North Sea drove the water up the rivers, and we had a terrible flood in the area around Hamburg. We were very concerned.

I happened to be touring the North German Mission at that particular time with President Howard Maycock. On Friday evening when we left Altona and drove through Hamburg on our way to Bremen, we passed along the levee and noticed that the water was rising. Some of the cars were already partially under water, and not much more than ten minutes after we passed the water came in and flowed over the very road that we had been traveling.

At that time we did not realize how serious conditions were. Although we knew that the water was high, we spent the night in Bremen, held our missionary conference there the next day, and as soon as I returned to Frankfurt by air I telephoned to find out how things were, for I heard that

President Maycock could not get back to Hamburg because the roads were under water.

I had reports from that area on Saturday night, and the president of the stake said they had things in hand and were working to care for the people but were concerned about some of the members. The amazing thing was the way our wonderful brethren there immediately sprang into action and took care of their own people. The president of that stake and his counselors with some of the members of the high council visited the bishops, checked on the Saints, found what was needed, and took care of them. They located and helped flood victims, for many of our people lost all their belongings. They lost their furniture, they lost their clothes, even the wallpaper was washed off the walls, and the homes were filled with slime from the floods, but miraculously all their lives were saved.

Some very remarkable things happened. President Panitsch told me that he was concerned about one elderly sister who was bedridden. He was afraid that the flood which covered much of Wilhelmsburg might have taken her life, because she could not move. However, the night before the flood came, she became a little more ill and was taken to a hospital and so was saved.

One of our sisters was concerned because in the middle of this flood, as the waters came rushing in, her children, whom she had held by the hand, were swept away from her by the floods, so she lost them and despaired of their lives. She was rescued and came in tears to her bishop, wanting to know what she could do for her children. But the children had been miraculously saved. They had clung to trees and had been rescued the following morning and were restored to her again, frightened but safe.

So you see, the local Saints helped one another. When the call went out to gather food and clothing, they brought so much material into the Altona branch house that the bishops had to tell the people, "We have enough. Don't bring any more." The sisters spent their time sorting the clothing (it was good clothing that was brought in) and making sure that all the people who received clothing had proper fit and suitable attire.

The local Saints helped one another. And the greatest testimony of unity for me, brothers and sisters, was to see how the presidents of the other German-speaking stakes sprang to the rescue. Berlin telephoned over and asked if they could help, and Switzerland and Stuttgart, without even bothering to telephone, started up their relief action and gathered sums of money, which to us were really large in terms of German marks, and sent that money to President Panitsch, offered food and clothing, and telephoned to ask if they could give more help.

So you see, they are working together, and those wonderful German and Swiss Saints in our European stakes held together as one people. It is a thrill to see such unity. I thought to myself, truly these stakes now are places of refuge and safety. Zion is where the pure in heart dwell, and these are true stakes of Zion. My heart swelled with pride for our Saints in Europe.

Conference Report, April 1962, pp. 54-55.

I Had Found It in Mr. Goddard's Grocery Store

I wish all boys could have had a mother such as I had. One day I came home eating an apple. Mother asked me where I got it. I told her I found it. She soon discovered that I had "found" it in Mr. Goddard's grocery store, and Mother insisted I take it back.

I protested that it was partly eaten, but at her urging I took the partly eaten apple back to Mr. Goddard and shamefully told him I had robbed his store. He phoned Mother to tell her I had brought it back and said he had seen me take it, but it was such a little thing he hadn't bothered to say anything about it. It wasn't a little thing to Mother. She loved us too much to have a thief in the family.

There is a phenomenon that accompanies dishonest persons. Before long they become very critical and tend to find fault with leaders who call their attention to their unrighteousness. Instead of repenting and changing their lives for the better, they tend to justify their own misdeeds by finding fault with their leaders. The Prophet Joseph Smith said:

"I will give you one of the Keys of the mysteries of the Kingdom. It is an eternal principle, that has existed with God from all eternity: That man who rises up to condemn others, finding fault with the Church, saying that they are out of the way, while he himself is righteous, then know assuredly, that that man is in the high road to apostasy; and if he does not repent, will apostatize, as God lives." (Joseph Fielding Smith, comp., *Teachings of the Prophet Joseph Smith*, pp. 156-57.)

Conference Report, April 1970, p. 91.

MATTHEW COWLEY

Elder Cowley was born on August 2, 1897, at Preston, Idaho, the son of Matthias F. Cowley and Abbie Hyde. He was called to serve a mission in New Zealand when just seventeen years old. He received a law degree from George Washington University.

On July 13, 1922, while still studying in Washington, D.C., he returned home to be married in the Salt Lake Temple to Elva Eleanor Taylor. Their marriage was performed by President George Albert Smith, then a member of the Council of the Twelve.

In 1938 Elder Cowley was called to preside over the New Zealand Mission.

On October 5, 1945, Brother Cowley was sustained a member of the Council of the Twelve as the Church met in solemn assembly in its semiannual conference. In this conference, President George Albert Smith was sustained as the President of the Church, and his first call to the apostleship went to Brother Cowley.

On October 11, 1945, Elder Cowley was ordained an apostle, the sixty-fifth of this dispensation, by President Smith. A year later, a new position of responsibility among the General Authorities of the Church was created, and Elder Cowley was appointed to fill the position as president of the Pacific Islands missions. In this new assignment, he was given the responsibility of directing the affairs of the Church in the many missions of the Pacific.

In addition to his travels in the islands, he visited in the missions of the Orient and in Australia. He visited the Philippine Islands, Japan, and China, dedicating China once again for the preaching of the gospel.

At the time of his unexpected passing on December 13, 1953, he had become one of the most-loved men of his time.

Matthew Cowley Speaks (Deseret Book Co., 1971), pp. vii-xii.

We Are Fasting and Praying

I had an experience down here about fasting.

I have got two friends down here from New Zealand—a couple. They had never had any children, and they finally thought they had adopted one, but one day along came the father and said he wanted his child. Maybe you saw it in the newspaper. It was in the headlines covering quite a period of time. He said, "I never put that child in that home to be adopted, just to be cared for." He had two other children. His wife was a drunkard, and she left him and left the children. "Now she is back with me. She has reformed. We want our children back." This couple had one of them. Well, they had had that child so long it was one of the family, and so they had a long drawn-out litigation.

I was there at conference a couple of months ago. This couple was here. They came up after one of the meetings on Sunday. I said, "How is the case coming out? What is happening?"

They said, "Well, the final hearing is on Tuesday."

I said, "All right. Tomorrow morning I have an engagement for breakfast. After that I will fast all day Monday until Tuesday evening. You join me. We will fast for that child, and then whatever happens is right." So they shed a few tears and we fasted, and I never heard any more about it until general conference. The lawyer was at conference.

I said, "How did the case come out?"

He said, "Well, it was the strangest thing. I called the witness to take the witness stand, and I said, 'You tell the judge now what you are doing for this child, what kind of home you have, what its prospects are for the future, the husband's ability to care for it, his job, the money he is making, and everything.' That's what I intended her to say. But I said, 'Tell the court what you are doing for this child.' Do you know what she said? She said, 'We are fasting and praying.' Do you know what the judge did. He had to declare a recess. He didn't say a word. He went back in his chambers and spent a few minutes, and he came out, and he awarded this child to these two, this couple. They have been married in the temple and had it sealed to them."

Address at San Fernando Stake welfare meeting, March 24, 1952.

I'm Ready Now to Bless Your Boy

We have a mutual friend down in Honolulu, Sister Widstoe and I, a man who is a young bishop down there, very wealthy, and yet a young man with a lot of humility. He was called one day from the Queen's Hospital to come and bless a boy who had polio. A native sister had called him. He was her bishop, and she said, "Bishop, come up here, my boy is stricken with polio, and I want you to come up here and administer to him and bless him." All day she waited for him, and the bishop never showed up. All night he never showed up.

The next morning he never showed up, but early in the afternoon here he came. She turned loose on him. She called him everything she could think of. "You, my bishop, I call you and tell you my boy is here stricken with polio. And you your own boss. You have your cars, you have a beautiful yacht, you have everything you want; and your time is your own; and you don't show up. You just come now after a whole day."

After she had finished and couldn't think of anything more to call him, he smiled and said, "Well, after I hung up the receiver yesterday, I started to fast, and I've been fasting and praying for twenty-four hours. I'm ready now to bless your boy." At five o'clock that evening the boy was released from the hospital, entirely cured of his polio. "This kind goeth not out but by prayer and fasting."

Matthew Cowley Speaks, [Salt Lake City: Deseret Book Co., 1954], pp. 149-50.

What on Earth Will I Do?

When I was invited to come here, President Wilkinson suggested that I might talk a little bit about miracles. Well, it will be a miracle if I do. I had a particular assignment or instruction from President George Albert Smith when I was called to this position. He called me into his office one day and took hold of my hand, and while he was holding my hand and looking at me he said, "I want to say something to you, Brother Cowley."

I said, "Well, I'm willing to listen."

"This is just a particular suggestion to you, not to all the brethren but to you." He said, "Never write a sermon. Never write down what you are going to say."

I said, "What on earth will I do?"

He said, "You tell the people what the Lord wants you to tell them while you are standing on your feet."

I said, "That certainly is putting some responsibility on the Lord."

But I've tried to live up to that instruction. And I've had some great experiences.

Speeches of the Year, "Miracles," February 18, 1953, p. 2.

He Was An Unusual Boy

A few weeks ago I was called to the County Hospital in Salt Lake City by a mother. I didn't know her. She said her boy was dying from polio and asked if I would come down and give that boy a blessing. So I picked up a young bishop whom I generally take with me, for I think his faith is greater than mine, and I always like him along. We went down there, and here was this young lad in an iron lung, unconscious, his face rather a blackish color, with a tube in his throat; and they said he had a tube lower down in his abdomen. He had been flown in from an outlying community. The mother said to me, "This is an unusual boy. Not because he's my child, but he is an unusual boy." I think he was eight or nine years of age.

After they put the usual coverings on us, we went in, and we blessed that boy. It was one of those occasions when I knew as I laid my hands upon that lad that he was an unusual boy, and he had faith. Having faith in his faith, I blessed him to get well and promised him he would. I never heard any more about him until last Sunday. I was on my way to Murray to conference; I dropped in the County Hospital, and I asked if I might see the lad. The nurse said, "Certainly. Walk right down the hall." As I walked down the hall, out came the boy running to meet me. He ran up and asked, "Are you Brother Cowley?"

And I said, "Yes."

He said, "I want to thank you for that prayer." He added, "I was unconscious then, wasn't I?"

I replied, "You certainly were."

He said, "That's the reason I don't recognize you." Then he asked, "Come in my room; I want to talk to you." He was an unusual boy. Well, we went in the room. He still had a tube in his throat. I said, "How long are you going to have that tube there?"

He said, "Oh, two weeks. Two more weeks, and then I'm all well. How about another blessing?"

So I said, "Certainly." I blessed him again. I was in a hurry. I wanted to get out to my conference. But he stopped me and asked, "Hey, how about my partner in the next bed?" There was a young fellow about sixteen or seventeen.

I said, "What do you mean?"

He said, "Don't go without blessing him. He's my partner."

I said, "Sure." Then I asked the boy, "Would you like a blessing?"

He said, "Yes, sir. I'm a teacher in the Aaronic Priesthood in my ward." I blessed him, and then my little friend went and brought another fellow in. Here was another partner. And I blessed him.

Now, except ye believe as a child, you can't receive these blessings.

Speeches of the Year, "Miracles," February 18, 1953, pp. 2-3.

Fix Me Up, I Want to Go Home

I know one of our dearest friends in New Zealand who is now reaching the end of his life; he's only two years older than I, and it's entirely due to his eating habits. He owned a taxicab company out there in one of the cities; every cab in the town he owned. One day he was stricken and started to have a hemorrhage from the nose, which couldn't be stopped. So they took him to the hospital, and the doctors couldn't stop it. So they sent for his family, and they came to be there when he passed on. When the family was standing around and the nurses were still working on him, he said to one of the nurses, "You go to the phone, and call my switchboard at the taxi office, and tell the girl to send a couple of my drivers out here quick." Every driver of every cab he owned was an elder in the Church.

The nurse went to the switchboard and called her and said, "The big man wants you to send a couple of his drivers out here to the hospital fast." She knew what it meant, so out went two drivers. "Fix me up, I want to go home." Just like that you know. One anointed him, the other sealed the anointing, and he got up out of bed and went home. The hemorrhage had ceased immediately. It was the simplest thing in the world, wasn't it? He didn't have any doubt at all about the power of God to heal. Medicine had failed, medical science had failed, so with simple faith he had his taxi drivers bless him.

Matthew Cowley Speaks, p. 148.

Just As Miraculous As Raising the Dead

A little child who lives on "B" Street was hit by an automobile, down in American Fork. For seven months that child lay on that bed up there at home. It never spoke; it was unconscious, had to be fed intravenously. I was speaking down in the old Granite Tabernacle, for a Japanese girl's farewell. The girl was a hairdresser, and the mother of this child was one of her clients. So after the meeting, she came up and said to me, "I wonder if you would have time to come up and bless my little girl?" I said, "Yes, I would be glad to; where do you live?" She told me, and I said, "That's not far from where I live."

So the next day we went up. I called a young bishop and away we went. We went up there and saw this child. Now, I believe if I hadn't been among the natives down in the islands, I wouldn't have had a bit of faith. There was that child helpless, all crippled up. And after that I went up once in a great while; once or twice I went fasting. One day I picked up the telephone at home, and the mother said to me, "Just wait a minute." So I waited there a minute, and I heard a little voice say, "This is so and so." And it was that little girl.

Last summer she was baptized, and she asked me if I would baptize her. So I went down to the Tabernacle and baptized the little girl. Now she is going to school. Her vision isn't perfect yet, but it is coming back. She is walking, and she is playing. Now to me that was just as miraculous as raising the dead.

Matthew Cowley Speaks, pp. 150-51.

The Doctor Isn't Home

When I went over to New Zealand on my first mission, I had only been there a day or two when a nice sister came running to me. And she said, "Come over, please." I was all alone. I didn't have a companion. I went over to the home, and there was a little boy, ten or eleven, I guess. He had fallen from a tree. She said, "Fix him up. I said, "You ought to have a doctor." I had never administered to anybody in my life, never. She said, "The doctor isn't home. He is away from town. We don't need a doctor. You fix him."

Well, I got down. He lay on the floor. I anointed him, and I sealed the anointing. You know, I guess God wanted to humble me. The next day he was climbing trees again. Every bone had knit. It was only a few days after that that her husband was stricken with typhoid fever. I was scared to death. The water was bad. I was all alone, just a youngster. She called me into her husband. I got down and anointed and blessed him, and the next morning he came over to my house and visited with me. And he said, "If you are going anywhere now, you can go. I am well." I have never had experiences like that in all my life.

Address delivered at San Fernando Stake Conference, May 28, 1952.

The Mortgage Is Paid Off

Over in Colorado once, I was at stake conference, and I asked one of the elders quorum presidents how his elders were getting along as a quorum. I said, "Do you do anything to help one another?"

"Oh, yes, we don't do bad."

I said, "Well, what are you doing?"

He said, "Well, I can tell you this: we've got a member of our quorum in the hospital down in Santa Fe, New Mexico. He was a strong, vigorous young man, buying a beautiful farm—a hard worker with a lovely little family. He was going ahead, paying off his bills and his mortgage, when all of a sudden he was stricken." Ordinarily that would have been the end of the farm, the end of security of the family. The elders quorum president said to me, "That was our loss as much as it was a loss for his wife and children. So we took over, and we've gone out and operated that farm. It doesn't take much time with all of our tractors and all our equipment. The mortgage is paid off, and the family has a good income from the farm. All the man has to worry about is getting well, down there in that hospital."

Leadership Week Lectures, 1953, "Learning to Live through Better Use of Vocational Opportunities," June 19, 1953, p. 5.

You Do Not Owe That Much Tithing

I had a little mother, and I still have her, down in New Zealand. I knew her on my first mission when I was just a young boy. In those days she called me her son. When I went back to preside, she called me her father.

Now, on one occasion I called in, as I always did when I visited that vicinity, to see this grand little woman, then in her eighties and blind. She did not live in an organized branch, had no contact with the priesthood except as the missionaries visited there. We had no missionaries in those days. They were away at war.

I went in and greeted her in the Maori fashion. She was out in her back yard by her little fire. I reached forth my hand to shake hands with her, and I was going to rub noses with her. And she said, "Do not shake hands with me, Father."

I said, "Oh, that is clean dirt on your hands. I am willing to shake hands with you. I am glad to. I want to."

She said: "Not yet." Then she got on her hands and knees and crawled over to her little house. At the corner of the house there was a spade. She lifted up that spade and crawled off in another direction, measuring the distance she went. She finally arrived at a spot and started digging down into the soil with that spade. It finally struck something hard. She took out the soil with her hands and lifted out a fruit jar. She opened that fruit jar and reached down in it, took something out and handed it to me, and it turned out to be New Zealand money. In American money it would have been equivalent to one hundred dollars.

She said, "There is my tithing. Now I can shake hands with the priesthood of God."

I said, "You do not owe that much tithing."

She said, "I know it. I do not owe it now, but I am paying some in advance, for I do not know when the priesthood of God will get around this way again."

Conference Report, October 1948, pp. 159-60.

Then I Am Safe for Another Week

We had a young sailor who came into our home in New Zealand during the war. He was a convert to the Church. Before he left San Francisco, he had been ordained a priest. And we asked him about his life on board ship. He was the only member of the Church on this big transport.

He said, "Well, whenever we stop at a port, the fellows all come around and kid me and say, 'Come on, let's go out and have a good time, get on a binge, get some relaxation.' But I do not go. You know the reason I do not go? You know the reason I can stand up against those invitations and temptation?" He said, "It is because the captain on the ship on Sunday gives me a little room, and I go into that little room all by myself. I have that little serviceman's copy of the Book of Mormon, so I take a little water and a piece of bread. I open up that Book of Mormon to Moroni, and I get down on my knees. I bless the sacrament, and I pass it to myself." And he said, "Then I am safe for another week." He said, "Nobody on earth can tempt me." He was learning how to live, fast, but not learning fast living. Just remember, he was learning to live the simple life.

Leadership Week Lectures, June 19, 1953.

See What You Have Done For Me

I was down in the Southwest Indian Mission. I went into church one day, and a fine-looking Navajo woman came in. And the missionary said to me, "I want to introduce you to this sister." So he took me up and introduced me to her, and we had a little chat, the best we could. Then after meeting this young missionary came to me and said, "Well, I am glad you met her. A few months ago my companion and I went to the Navajo reservation. We went into a hogan. There lay this woman on her back, on a sheepskin. She had been there for six long years. She had never stood up. When we were about to leave, she said to us, 'Isn't there something you people do for people who are sick and afflicted?' I said, 'Yes.' She said, 'Will you please do it for me?' So we got down on our knees; one anointed her with oil, the other one sealed the anointing. After we left—we were only a short distance away—she came running out from the hogan and said, 'Come back and see what you have done for me.' She has been walking ever since."

Speeches of the Year, "Miracles," February 18, 1953, p. 10.

I Received a Message

I've learned a lot from these islanders that I see scattered around here. I see Albert Whaanga from New Zealand in the audience; I wish he'd teach you people how to rub noses. That's what we do down in New Zealand, you know. We don't really rub. You just press your forehead and your nose against the nose and forehead of the other person. It's a wonderful thing. You can always tell when they're keeping the Word of Wisdom down there. All you have to do is walk up and greet them and sniff a little bit, and you've got 'em! It would be a good practice to have over here. So if I ever come up to one of you some day and say I'd like to rub noses with you, you'll know I'm suspecting something.

These natives live close to God. They have some kind of power. I guess it's just because they accept miracles as a matter of course. They never doubt anything. They used to scare me. Someone would come up and say, "Brother Cowley, I've had a dream about you."

I'd say, "Don't tell me. I don't want to hear about it."

"Oh, it was a good one."

"All right. Tell me."

And they'd tell me something. Now I remember when President Rufus K. Hardy of the First Council of the Seventy passed away. I was walking along the street of one of the cities in New Zealand, and one of our native members came up—a lady.

She said to me, "President Hardy is dead."

I said, "Is that so? Have you received a wire?"

She said, "No. I received a message, but I haven't received any wire." She repeated, "He's dead. I know."

Well, I always believed them when they told me those things. When I got back to headquarters, I wasn't there long when here came a cablegram which said that President Hardy had passed away the night before. But she knew that without any cablegram. She told me about it.

I got out of my car once in the city. I got out to do some window-shopping to get a little rest from driving. I walked around, and finally I went around a corner, and there stood a native woman and her daughter. The mother said to the daughter, "What did I tell you?"

I said, "What's going on here?"

The daughter said, "Mother said if we'd stand here for fifteen minutes you'd come around the corner." Now she didn't have any radio set with her, just one in her heart where she received the impression.

After President Hardy died, we had a memorial service for him. I'll never forget the native who was up speaking, saying what a calamity it was to the mission to lose this great New Zealand missionary who could do so much for them as one of the Authorities of the Church. He was talking along that line, and all of a sudden he stopped and looked around at me and said, "Wait a minute. There's nothing to worry about. When President Cowley gets home, he'll fill the first vacancy in the Council of the Twelve Apostles, and we'll still have a representative among the Authorities of the Church." Then he went on talking about President Hardy. When I arrived home the following September, I filled the first vacancy in the Quorum of the Twelve. Now did that just happen by chance?

Speeches of the Year, "Miracles," February 18, 1953, p. 7.

Medical Science Had Laid the Burden Down

A little over a year ago a couple came into my office carrying a little boy. The father said to me, "My wife and I have been fasting for two days, and we've brought our little boy up for a blessing. You are the one we've been sent to."

I said, "What's the matter with him?"

They said he was born blind, deaf, and dumb, had no coordination of his muscles, couldn't even crawl at the age of five years. I said to myself, this is it. I had implicit faith in the fasting and the prayers of those parents. I blessed the child, and a few weeks later I received a letter: "Brother Cowley, we wish you could see our little boy now. He's crawling. When we throw a ball across the floor, he races after it on his hands and knees. He can see. When we clap our hands over his head, he jumps. He can hear." Medical science had laid the burden down. God had taken over. The little boy was rapidly recovering, or really getting what he'd never had.

<small>Speeches of the Year, "Miracles," February 18, 1953, p. 8.</small>

Send for the Elders

I was called to a home in a little village in New Zealand one day. There the Relief Society sisters were preparing the body of one of our Saints. They had placed his body in front of the Big House, as they call it, the house where the people came to wail and weep and mourn over the dead, when in rushed the dead man's brother.

He said, "Administer to him."

And the young natives said, "Why, you shouldn't do that; he's dead."

"You do it!"

This [was the] same old man that I had with me when his niece was so ill was there. The younger native got down on his knees, and he anointed the dead man. Then this great old sage got down and blessed him and commanded him to rise. You should have seen the Relief Society sisters scatter. And he sat up, and he said, "Send for the elders; I don't feel very well." Now, of course, all of that was just psychological effect on that dead man. Wonderful, isn't it—this psychological effect business? Well, we told him he had just been administered to, and he said: "Oh, that was it." He said, "I was dead. I could feel life coming back into me just like a blanket unrolling." Now, he outlived the brother that came in and told us to administer to him.

<small>Speeches of the Year, "Miracles," February 18, 1953, p. 9.</small>

Give Him His Vision

I've told the story about the little baby nine months old who was born blind. The father came up with him one Sunday and said, "Brother Cowley, our baby hasn't been blessed yet; we'd like you to bless him."

I said, "Why have you waited so long?"

"Oh, we just didn't get around to it."

Now, that's the native way; I like that. Just don't get around to doing things! Why not live and enjoy it? I said, "All right, what's the name?" So he told me the name, and I was just going to start when he said, "By the way, give him his vision when you give him a name. He was born blind." Well, it shocked me, but then I said to myself, why not? Christ told his disciples when he left them they could work miracles. And I had faith in that father's faith. After I gave that child its name, I finally got around to giving it its vision. That boy's about twelve years old now. The last time I was back there I was afraid to inquire about him. I was sure he had gone blind again. That's the way my faith works sometimes. So I asked the branch president about him. And he said, "Brother Cowley, the worst thing you ever did was to bless that child to receive his vision. He's the meanest kid in the neighborhood, always getting into mischief." Boy, I was thrilled about that kid getting into mischief!

Speeches of the Year, "Miracles," February 18, 1953, pp. 9-10.

JAMES A. CULLIMORE

Elder James A. Cullimore was born January 17, 1906, to Albert Lorenzo and Luella Keetch Cullimore, and was a native of Lindon, Utah.

He was sustained to the First Quorum of the Seventy on October 1, 1976.

Elder Cullimore lived in Oklahoma City for more than thirty years, eventually operating his own furniture business.

He became the first president of the Oklahoma Stake when it was organized in 1960. He later served as president of the Central British Mission.

As a young man he served a mission in California. He was graduated from Brigham Young University, where he was student body president. He married Grace Gardner in the Salt Lake Temple, and they are the parents of a son and two daughters.

Elder Cullimore passed away in Salt Lake City on June 14, 1986.

This Is Where You Are Supposed to Be

In 1937 we moved to Oklahoma City, where I worked for a large department store as divisional merchandise manager. After a few years the owner of the business passed away and his widow took over the management of the business. I became somewhat dissatisfied with my employment and began to look elsewhere.

About this time Elder Joseph F. Merrill, an apostle, was touring the mission, and as he visited Oklahoma City, he stayed in our home. We sought his advice as to our moving. Sister Cullimore visited with him at great length one morning, expressing her concern as to the children's associating with nonmembers almost entirely. They were getting to the age of dating, and she was concerned that they had no members of their own age to associate with. We were concerned that they might marry out of the Church.

Brother Merrill said to us, "Don't worry about it. This is where you are supposed to be. The Lord has directed you here and this is where you are needed. There are plenty of folks out west that can take care of the responsibilities there. You are needed here." He said, "Don't be worried about your children marrying out of the Church. Just make sure that you teach them the gospel, have a good home life, see that they go to their meetings, and then send them to a Church school, and they'll marry in the Church."

We listened to this direction and gave heed to it, really never expecting things to move quite as fast as they did. But the very next day after he was there, as I went out to lunch I met a real estate man whom I had asked to keep his eyes open for a building that we might rent to go into business for ourselves. This had been several months earlier and I'm sure he had not taken it too seriously and had done nothing about it, but as I sat and visited with him this day at lunch, he said, "I've just been over to your store to offer them a building to rent to open a residential store in the city."

I asked him where it was and he told me and I said, "That's exactly the location I have been looking for. Why haven't you let me know about it?"

He said, "Well, it's yours if you want it; they didn't take it."

So within three days we had made our decision to rent the building and go into business for ourselves. We started out in a very modest way, but the business mushroomed and prospered and we felt strongly the hand of the Lord in this direction. Because of our business and the success of it, we were able to help many of the branches get buildings and move on faster than they otherwise would have done.

We also saw the fulfillment of the other advice Brother Merrill gave, that of the children marrying in the temple. We have three children, all of whom have married in the temple and are active and faithful in the Church, and even though none of them really found their mates at the Church school, they all attended Church schools. We are grateful for their faithfulness and the fulfillment of the promise made by a servant of the Lord.

"*Dump the Sand from Your Shoes*," BYU Speeches of the Year, May 3, 1967, p. 5.

But If You Put Him in Cold Water...

Every day I am more aware that it is the little things that we really need to be aware of and repent of in our lives. For the little things build into the big things and then often it is too late. Repentance applies to any act that is wrong, to any untruth, any error, no matter how insignificant we may think it. As they are detected, no matter how simple, they should be checked and repented of and cast aside and never be permitted to build into the things of major consequence.

The devices of Satan are subtle. He is cunning in his approach. He would be discovered readily if his enticements were all of major importance. But the simple, insignificant wrong acts often are accepted and passed unnoticed in our sense of right and wrong.

There is an old saying that "You can't kill a frog by dropping him into hot water." As you drop him into the hot water, he reacts so quickly that he immediately jumps out unharmed. But if you put him in cold water and gradually warm it up until it is scalding hot, you have him cooked before he knows it. The encroachment of bad habits in our lives is very much like this.

"*Dump the Sand from Your Shoes*," BYU Speeches of the Year, May 3, 1967.

The Sand Kept Getting into My Shoes

An interesting experience is related by Mr. Harleigh M. Rosenberger: "Several years ago a man was being interviewed on a radio. He had started to walk across the United States on foot, from California to New York. He had reached a point halfway across. Reporters asked him about his experience. Finally, the question came, 'Sir, what would you say has been your most difficult experience so far?'

"The traveler thought long. Through his mind went the toilsome climb over mountain passes; hot dry stretches of desert. Sun. Wind. Then he said quietly, 'I guess my greatest problem was that the sand kept getting into my shoes.'

"So that was it. The sand in his shoes. Not some great crisis that he had faced. Not some danger that had almost taken his life. But sand. Sand that wore blisters on the soles of his feet. Sand that ground its way between the pores of his skin and irritated constantly, that made every step an agony. Sand in his shoes.

"Life is like that. It is not always the great crisis in life that crushes. Not always the deepest sorrows or the great disappointments. Most often, it is the constant irritation of small things—things insignificant in themselves. We can stand up to the big things of life. But the petty things can often cause our downfall, until we say ofttimes it is just one thing after another. For the little things have a way of wearing down our inner reserves of strength."

"Dump the Sand from Your Shoes," BYU Speeches of the Year, May 3, 1967.

I Forgot to Tell You, But He Rose Again

The story is told of a man walking down a street in Chicago who came to a store window where there was displayed a beautiful picture of the crucifixion. As he stood gazing spellbound at the vivid picture story, he suddenly became conscious that at his side stood a little boy. The boy too was gazing at the picture, and his tense expression made the man know that the crucifixion had really gripped the eager little soul. Touching the boy on the shoulder, the man said, "Sonny, what does it mean?"

"Don'cha know?" he answered, his face full of the marvel of the man's ignorance. "That there man is Jesus, and them others is Roman soldiers, and the woman crying is his mother, and," he added, "they killed him."

The man was loath to leave the window, but he could not tarry always at the tragic scene, so he turned away and walked down the street. In a few moments he heard pattering footsteps, and there came rushing toward him the little boy.

"Say, mister!" he exclaimed breathlessly. "I forgot to tell you, but he rose again!"

Yes, he rose again. The advent on earth of the Redeemer is of less importance than the conquest of death and the grave, for it was only by rising from the grave that he could redeem the world. Hence, his resurrection signals the redemption of man-kind and becomes one of the greatest of all occasions for every child of God.

Conference Report, April 1968, pp. 36-37.

It Was a Feeling That She Had

I remember so well the story of a good sister in Barry, South Wales. She and her husband had prayed on numerous occasions for the Lord to direct them in the work. They were conscious of the fact that the things they were doing were not very useful. They were accomplishing nothing; they had no purpose in life; and as she stared out in the starlit heavens one evening she prayed to the Lord that he would guide her in the work and lead her to accomplish more than they were accomplishing.

Then the next day two young men knocked on the door. At first she did not recognize the answer of the Lord to her. As they gave her the door approach and introduced her to the gospel, she listened attentively, then quickly told them she was not interested, and they went on their way.

As soon as they had left, she felt something had gone with them, and she sent her daughter out into the rain to find them. After a few attempts, they returned, and she related to me later that she had the same feeling when they returned as she had before they had left. She said it was not what they had said, for she did not remember really a thing they had said, but it was a feeling that she had when they were there that accompanied them and bore witness to her.

"The Latter-day Harvest," BYU Speeches of the Year, May 9, 1972, p. 3.

Beware of the Mormons

I was interested in listening to the story of a new branch president in Bandung, Indonesia, just two months ago. He was a wonderful man, so qualified and excited in his newfound religion. I asked him how he came to be interested in the Church. He told me a very interesting story.

He had been to the doctor, and, after the doctor had completed the examination, she had said, "You look like a good Christian man."

He said, "No, I am a good Buddhist, a very good Buddhist."

But the doctor said, "I still think you should investigate some of the good Christian religions, for you would be a good Christian. There are many here in the city that you could investigate." Then she said, "There is only one thing I need to warn you about. Beware of the Mormons."

Well, he had never heard of the Mormons, and this had aroused his curiosity. He went home and looked at the encyclopedia that night and got his first understanding of the Mormons, and it was not a very good account. Still, he was curious and looked further. It was only a day or two until the missionaries knocked at his door, and in three or four weeks he and his wife and son had joined the Church. And, even though he had not known of the gospel before and his manner of worship and understanding of things religious were entirely different, he made the transition beautifully.

As I listened to this wonderful new member of the Church relate his story, the thought occurred to me that even though he had been a non-Christian, the message of the restored gospel had appealed to him, and the Spirit had borne witness to him of the truth. And I thought, Why not? When the Prophet received an answer to his prayer in the grove that day, he had asked the Lord which of all the churches he should join. And the Lord had told him that he should join none of them. And, as I remember, I don't think he made any exceptions as to whether they were Christian or non-Christian.

I had assumed, when first given some responsibility for this basically non-Christian area, it would be necessary to convert an individual to Christianity and then to Mormonism. It was rather interesting to observe that this was not the case. The same general approach is used in teaching the non-Christian as the Christian.

"The Latter-day Harvest," *BYU Speeches of the Year*, May 9, 1972, pp. 3-4.

RICHARD L. EVANS

From 1930 until his death in 1971, Richard L. Evans delivered the "Spoken Word" on the nationwide broadcast of "Music and the Spoken Word" with the Tabernacle Choir each Sunday from Temple Square in Salt Lake City. He was the producer and writer as well as the "voice" on the broadcast.

Born in Salt Lake City in 1906, the youngest of nine children, Richard Evans lived three years in Europe. He received his B.A., M.A., and LL.D. degrees from the University of Utah, having majored in English and economics. He was the author of seventeen books.

Elder Evans married Alice Thornley Evans. They are the parents of four sons.

He was ordained a member of the Council of the Twelve Apostles on October 8, 1953, and fulfilled many duties across the globe, in addition to his service with the Tabernacle Choir.

Elder Evans passed away in Salt Lake City on November 1, 1971.

We Cannot Make a Blade of Grass

Some days ago I spent some time with a young man who was troubled. He did not like the way our Father in heaven was running the world. He said, "We need to know more."

Well, I agreed with him. We do need to know more. I should like to know all the answers. I am sure we all would. But, I said, "Let us begin with what we know. I think we can agree that there are some things we do know. What are we doing with them? Let us begin with the Ten Commandments, and also the two great commandments:

Thou shalt love the Lord thy God with all thy heart, and with all thy soul, and with all thy mind.

This is the first and great commandment.

And the second is like unto it, Thou shalt love thy neighbor as thyself. (Matthew 22:37-39.)

"Do you know anyone who is keeping them in their fullness? Just for example, do you know anyone who literally and always loves his neighbor as himself? I agree we need to know more, but also we need more to use more of what we do know."

The Lord has set up the objectives. He has given us a few simple rules. He has given us freedom; he has given us the right of choice, and what we shall become will depend, beyond his saving grace, on what we do with what we know.

And in replying to this young man, I could not refrain from observing that even though I were to agree with him, there are some things I would do differently from my point of view. I reminded him that we—he and I—cannot make a worm, and we cannot make a blade of grass, and who were we to dictate to the Creator in our small wisdom?

One thing he was troubled about was the necessity for faith: Why could he not know by sight or sound of the existence of God himself? "Why can't I see him? Why doesn't he tell these things to me? Why do I have to live by faith?"

There are people who have not had to live by faith who have found themselves in serious trouble. There are those to whom the Lord God has spoken who have made grievous errors.

Let us take the case of Lucifer, who lived with his Father. He did not have to have faith as to the existence of his Father in heaven, but what did his knowledge do for him? He was brilliant, but he lacked humility. He was arrogant and overly ambitious. He wanted to usurp his Father's power, and he wanted to do things in his own way. He wanted to change the commandments, to change the rules, and to run the kingdom according to his own view of things. So it is not always just not knowing that gets in our way. With his brilliance, humility would have saved Lucifer, but that he did not seem to have.

Conference Report, April 1957, pp. 12-13.

When I Have Said What I Know to Be True

There were some events associated with the dedication of the London Temple which I should like to relate also. Our President [David O. McKay] went there, and we had arranged a press conference for him on the late afternoon following what was to have been the morning of his arrival, thinking that he would have time for rest and still time to face that arduous task. But his plane was three hours late, or more. He had been up all the night before with those who accompanied him, President and Sister Smith and Brother Reiser, and there was no time for rest; and he faced that battery of some thirty or forty newsmen representing the great London dailies and others of the British Empire and the wire services, and the BBC television camera.

They pressed many questions, difficult and sometimes tenacious and penetrating questions, as is the function of alert and seasoned newsmen. He met them forthrightly, with some declarations of affirmation as to things we should know and how we could be assured of knowing them. They were respectful, but one always wonders what will happen the morning after when what was said appears in print, with the reporter's personal color or understanding or misunderstanding on it. Some of us worried about it considerably.

I saw the President in the lobby of the hotel that evening and expressed some of my concern, and he made a very significant statement. I do not know whether he remembers it or not, but I think I shall not forget it. He said, "When I have said what I know to be true, I do not worry about the consequences."

Conference Report, October 1958, pp. 58-59.

I Was Sufficiently Interested

A great man has been in our midst here for a few days, one of the notable men of medicine, Sir Alexander Fleming, whom we have had the pleasure in this community of meeting and hearing on one or two occasions. He told the story of how, in working in a laboratory in a London hospital back in 1928, he observed the action of an accidental mold that had drifted into his laboratory from some source and which had an arresting effect on some germ colonies that were in the culture in one of his petri dishes. His statement, as he recorded it in his diary, was this: "I was sufficiently interested to pursue the subject. The appearance of the culture plant was such that I thought it should not be neglected." Thus, penicillin was discovered and put to immeasurable human benefit.

"I was sufficiently interested to pursue the subject." Well, with a mold so common, so accessible, one wonders why someone did not see it sooner, why someone did not "pursue the subject" sooner. That the world should go so long without such a discovery from such a common and available source would seem to be but a further indication that there is ever before us an infinity of undiscovered things, that opportunities are limitless, and that "revelation" of this kind is continuous, as is direct revelation from our Father in heaven.

The songs of birds that are all around us, we often do not hear. Two enterprising scientists not long ago made some "visual recordings" of bird songs with an audio-spectrograph, so that the human eye would "see" the music that the birds were making, but the human ear could not hear it as it reached above the range of "normal" human hearing.

Who knows what unseen and unheard things may be all around us? There are limitless possibilities; there is infinity before us, and revelation must be continuous.

Conference Report, April 1954, p. 84.

No Greater Mission

I believe there is no greater mission field, however much we may emphasize others, than there is at home and in the home.

Night before last, I read in the newspaper of a mother who had been chosen as Utah's Mother of 1947 and who had fifty-eight living descendants. I remember reading of an elderly patriarch in Utah County, some years ago, who was then living but has since died, and who then had one hundred forty-eight living descendants. I recall having seen a picture of President George F. Richards and his excellent family on the occasion of his eightieth birthday. They then numbered, as I recall, more than ninety descendants living, and they no doubt have added many more since then in these past five or six years.

What would have been the cumulative result if, many years ago, someone hadn't done his duty in the Church and had allowed one of these three whom I have mentioned to become indifferent or estranged from the Church early in life or to become offended for some reason?

When we are dealing with the life of a boy or girl, we are not dealing with an individual only. We are dealing with a whole posterity, and not with time only, but with life eternal. And there is no greater mission mothers and fathers can perform than to keep their sons and daughters close to them and close to the Church, and no greater mission that we at home can perform than to see that no one has cause for offense because of us, and that no one is allowed to lapse into indifference and inactivity, and that no one who is now inactive fails to be labored with, with all that we have to give; because we are not dealing with an individual only: we are dealing with generations and with ultimate consequences of which we have no conception.

I plead with you, my brothers and sisters, to consider this fact, and whenever you look at an individual, don't think of him just as he is, but think of the potentialities of his life and of generations to come—and never give him up.

Conference Report, April 1947, p. 97.

Because My Father Said So

I remember the words of a beloved stake president, and I thank him for the thought he left with me some months ago. He said, "I used to ride the range with my father, looking for lost sheep or cattle. And as we would mount a ridge we would look off into a distant hollow or a clump of trees, and my father would say, 'There they are.'" But this stake president said, "My father could see farther than I could, and often I couldn't see them.

But I knew they were there because my father said so."

There are many things, my beloved brethren and sisters, that I know and you know are there, because our Father said so. And I know that he lives, that he made us in his image, that he sent his divine Son, our Savior, to show us the way of life and redeem us from death. I know that he will enter into our lives as fully as we let him, and that his church and gospel and way of life are on earth and here with us, and that we will realize our highest possibilities if we accept the counsels God has given, and that we will fall somewhat, somewhere short of what we might have been or might have had if we run contrary to his commandments.

"Should the Commandments Be Rewritten?", *Ensign*, December 1971, p. 59.

That's Statistics for You

I should like to close with one story, and I think maybe this is a good time to tell it. It is my favorite story on statistics. I have told it in a number of places. It is not my story, but it belongs to Brother Roscoe Eardley, and if I violate the spirit of it I believe he is here and he can correct me. I may violate the statistics, but not the spirit, I hope.

Knowing of my interest in the subject, he stopped me one day and said, "I have the latest story on statistics for you. We were coming from California by automobile and we had all been over the road a number of times and were somewhat bored with it, and, as travelers often do to pass time, we began counting service stations. And we counted one for almost every mile along that eight hundred-mile journey. But that is not the story. We were so busy counting service stations that we ran out of gas!"

I did not sympathize with him too much because he had already told me there was one service station for about every mile. Then he said, "That's statistics for you. Where we ran out it was about fifteen miles to the nearest gas pump!"

Now I hope, brethren, in all our activities and responsibilities in this church that we do not become so absorbed in our statistics that we presume they are the end rather than merely the indicators, the barometer rather than the storm. What is on paper means nothing except as it is a symbol of what happens in the life of a man or a woman or a boy or a girl.

Conference Report, April 1948, p. 169.

I Still Plant Cherry Trees

I recall a reported statement, attributed, as I remember it, to President Wilford Woodruff. Some of the brethren of his time are said to have approached him (they had their troubles also) and to have inquired of him as to when he felt the end would be—when would be the coming of the Master? These, I think, are not his exact words, but they convey the spirit of his reported reply: "I would live as if it were to be tomorrow—but I am still planting cherry trees!"

I think we may well take this as a page for our own book and live as if the end might be tomorrow—and still plant cherry trees! In worrying about things that are beyond our reach, we should not overlook our opportunities with our own families and friends; in worrying about possible eventualities we should not neglect the things that need to be done here and now, and that are within our reach, the things for which we are immediately responsible; we should not neglect our present opportunities and obligations.

I should like to close with a statement of William Allen White: "I am not afraid of tomorrow, for I have seen yesterday, and I love today."

Conference Report. April 1950, pp. 105-106.

Sometimes I Do Things I Know I Shouldn't Do

About all we can take with us, after all, are the knowledge and character we have acquired, the intelligence we have developed or improved upon, the service we have given, the lessons we have learned, and the blessed assurance that we may have our life and loved ones, always and forever—as assured us by a wise and kindly Father whose children we all are. And knowing him, and what he is to us (and what we are to one another), what his purpose is in sending us here from his presence, is one of the surest safeguards against loneliness and feelings of frustration.

Some few evenings ago, I sat at dinner by the side of a distinguished, successful industrialist, who told me simply and in a few sentences how he faced the heavy problems of his life and met the decisions of each day:

"When I get up in the morning," he said, "I often feel that I can't face it, but as I get down on my knees and say simply 'God help me to do what I have to do this day,' strength comes, and I feel that I am equal to it. And I think of him as my Father, and talk to him as simply and directly as I used to talk to my father when he was here."

And then he added: "Sometimes I do things I know I shouldn't do. But when I do, I don't lie to God about my motives. I know it's no use; I know he knows my heart, my thoughts. I know what I have done, and he knows what I have done. And I don't try to deceive him or myself."

I was mellowed and humbled by the direct and simple spirit of this friend with whom I sat the other evening. He was not of my faith, but in my own earnest belief, he could not have talked to God with so much satisfaction or assurance if he had thought of him merely as a force, or as an ineffable essence, the nature and purpose of which he knew nothing—or at least nothing that would bring to him the assured feeling that he was in fact talking to his father.

Conference Report, October 1954, pp. 86-87.

The Spirit of All Truth

A cherished friend of mine, whose life paralleled mine for many years, up to a few years ago, when there was a parting of the ways, is now in one of America's greatest institutions of learning and has achieved international eminence in his scientific field. A few weeks ago he wrote me and said: "I am conducting researches in many fields, and I am just beginning to learn the high cost of finding out the truth about anything." And he continued: "The problem is so complex that all we can do is arrive at half-truths and first approximations."

I wrote him back and said: "It must be a great comfort to you, in your work, to know that you are a member of a church that will accept everything of truth that you ever find in your researches, in whatever field of thought or activity, and all that we ask of you is to pursue them beyond that stage of half-truth and first approximations of which you have spoken and conduct them to their final end, where there will be no question about their eternal verity to that point where the generations to come will not of necessity repudiate them."

I have a strong feeling that our young people who go into our universities and colleges should have before them constantly the promise of Moroni, that "by the power of the Holy Ghost ye may know the truth of all things," which is repeated in substance in the Doctrine and Covenants to the effect that "the Holy Ghost showeth all things and teacheth the peaceable things of the kingdom."

I never remember having gone into an examination of any consequence in my life without making it a matter of prayer. I know that the young man or young woman who approaches any problem in the academic field, or any other field, would have a great advantage if he would keep as his constant companion the spirit of our Father in heaven, which would give him an active sense of warm assurance when he was in the presence of truth and would give him a contrary feeling when he was not in the presence of truth. It wouldn't give him knowledge without study, or discovery without search, or truth without effort, but, granted that he pursued his work intelligently and diligently, he would have a great advantage in all of his findings and doings, academically and otherwise, if he made the spirit of all truth his constant guide.

Conference Report, October 1940, pp. 59 60.

MARION D. HANKS

Elder Marion D. Hanks is an emeritus member of the First Quorum of the Seventy. His service has taken him to many nations.

Throughout his life he has been prominent in civic affairs, particularly in the field of youth development. He has spoken at youth conferences throughout the world and was a featured speaker at the White House Conference on Children and Youth.

He served for many years in the leadership of Temple Square. As a young man he filled a two-year mission for the Church in the northern United States, and he also spent several years in England and Europe in mission leadership there.

During World War II Elder Hanks served aboard a submarine chaser in the Pacific. In recent years he has visited servicemen at their bases in many parts of the world.

Elder Hanks married Maxine Christensen in the Hawaiian Temple, and they are the parents of four daughters and one son.

Kneel Down, Son

Let me give you an example. I sat at a stake conference where a returned missionary bore his testimony. He had but a short time and he chose to use one idea. He thanked God for a great, humble mother, and gave his reason. He said that as a high school boy, he had been sorely tried by the illness and then death of his little sister whom he had loved greatly and who had been the darling of the family, being the last of them. Their father had died. The little girl grew ill, and in spite of prayers and administrations and fasting and much concern, worsened and died in the night. The boy went into his room, locked the door, and sobbed out his broken heart to the walls because he was not willing to do it to the God whom he could not now honestly approach. In his rebellion and anger at a God, if there were one who would permit such a thing to happen to them, he cried out in rebellion. He said he would never pray again, would never go to church again, and could never have any confidence again in a God who would permit this to happen. And in his immature but sincere sorrow, he made some rather serious covenants with himself. He stayed awake the rest of the night, apprehensive about an experience he anticipated. It was their custom, as it is in so many, though not enough, Latter-day Saint homes, to kneel morning and evening with the children around the mother, to thank God for the goodness of his blessings.

He waited for that moment, knowing what he had to say, but fearing it. When his mother said, "Come, children," he said, "No."

She said, "Kneel down, son."

He said, "No, I will not kneel down, and I will never kneel down again."

She said, as I remember his words, and I was deeply touched as were we all, "Son, you're the oldest child in this home. You are the only man in the house, and if I ever needed a man, I need one now. You kneel down."

He knelt down, still rebellious, but because his mother, the idol of his heart, needed him; and he began for the first time to think in terms of her broken heart and her sorrow. So he knelt, but he said to himself, "I wonder what she's going to thank God for this morning." And his mother, knowing as she must have, the questions in his mind and the minds of the other children, taught them the gospel on their knees that morning. She thanked God for what the family knew, for the blessing of eternal ties, for direction and purpose and guidance and convictions as to the future.

She thanked God that they had been blessed with this wonderful, angelic child who had brought so much to them and who was to be theirs, always. And out of her mother's heart, knowing the desperate, critical nature of the moment, taught her own children what there was to thank God for under conditions of such stress.

As the boy stood, a successful, dedicated Latter-day Saint who had filled an honorable, difficult mission, he thanked God for a mother who was a heroine, who had the qualities of heroism in every conceivable degree.

BYU Speeches of the Year, "Heroism," 1958-59, pp. 3-4.

Say, Hanks, Do You Believe in Jesus Christ?

The Christmas story that I want to mention occurred in the middle of the summer some years ago, at a naval training center. The man opposite me in the room had the many stripes on his arm that signified long and distinguished service; I was an apprentice seaman in boot camp. Nonetheless, Commander Hamilton, as he greeted me at the door, was most gracious. He called me "Mr. Hanks," seated me with cordiality, and we talked as equals. He had invited me to discuss the possibility of a chaplaincy. I was quick to tell him that because of a mission, I had not finished an academic degree and didn't qualify under the Navy's standards. He as quickly responded that he felt he could do something about getting that requirement waived, all things else being favorable. After a little more conversation, this rangy, fine looking man, who had been over the bow of the Yorktown on a line when she was sunk shortly before, who had everything about him that was manly and attractive to a man and was a chaplain and servant of the Lord, not of our faith, said to me, "Before I recommend you to the Chief of Chaplains, do me a favor, please. Talk to me about your experience in your Church, about what you think may help me recommend you as qualified to represent the Lord in the military chaplaincy."

And so I began, and, I want to protest, with earnestness and honesty, to try to tell him what I felt, out of our common experience in the Church, might qualify me to serve in that very significant role. He who had been so courteous and so kind began to be fidgety, and I quickly knew, as we do when we seek to communicate person-to-person, that I wasn't making it, that I was losing. And I became a little more anxious, trying to tell him what there is, this stage-by-stage opportunity in the Church for a young person to develop the quality to be a servant of God. I told him from the beginning—the early two and a half minute talks, the scouting, the deacon opportunity, the Sunday School teaching, and the mission.

After a time his demeanor completely changed. He finally interrupted me. He said, Say, Hanks, do you believe in Jesus Christ?"

I said, "Yes, sir. Everything I believe relates to Jesus Christ. The name of the Church that I belong to is his name. My faith revolves around him as my Savior."

He, looking at his watch, said, "Well, you have been talking seven minutes and you haven't said so." I think I have not made that mistake again.

BYU Speeches of the Year, "Was He Relevant?", December 17, 1968, pp. 2-3.

Boy, We Really Have a Swell Bathroom, Haven't We?

He who believes knows that he belongs. But he also needs to feel himself an important and accepted part of a group. Young people want and deserve parents and a family they can be proud of. Their capacity to become worthwhile persons is strongly affected by the absence or presence of such a family and by their own acceptance of the challenge to be a contributing, responsible member of it. The influence of a good family is well-captured by this account from an unknown source:

"It was a gorgeous October day. My husband Art and I were down at the boat landing helping our friend Don drag his skiff up on the beach. Art remarked wistfully that it would be a long time before next summer, when we could all start sailing again. 'You folks ought to take up skiing like our family and have fun the year round,' Don said.

"'Doesn't that get pretty expensive?' I asked.

"Don straightened up and smiled. 'It's funny,' he said. 'We live in an old-fashioned house—legs on the tub, that sort of thing. For years we have been saving up to have the bathroom done over. But every winter we take the money out of the bank and go on a couple of family skiing trips. Our oldest boy is in the army now, and he often mentions in his letters what a great time we had on those trips. You know, I can't imagine his writing home, "Boy, we really have a swell bathroom, haven't we?"'

Conference Report, April 1969, p. 57.

HOWARD W. HUNTER

President Howard W. Hunter became the fourteenth president of The Church of Jesus Christ of Latter-day Saints on June 5, 1994. Although his presidency lasted less than a year, he left a lasting mark as he challenged Church members to become temple worthy and invited members who had been offended to return to full activity.

As president, he dedicated two temples and traveled to Nauvoo, Illinois to commemorate the 150th anniversary of the martyrdom of Joseph and Hyrum Smith.

He was a prominent Southern California lawyer and businessman before his call to the apostleship on October 10, 1959.

He was born in Boise, Idaho, November 14, 1907, son of John William and Nellie Marie Rasmussen Hunter. After attending elementary schools and graduating from high school in Boise, he moved to California in 1928.

In June 1931, Elder Hunter married Clara May Jeffs in the Salt Lake Temple. They had three children. She died on October 9, 1983. He later married Inis Bernice Egan on April 12, 1990.

President Hunter passed away in Salt Lake City on March 3, 1995.

There Is Danger in Looking Backward

Not long ago we were traveling through the air so high above the white clouds that they looked like a blanket of snow beneath us. The sky was blue, and the sun was shining, and then we commenced our descent for landing. As we came down through the clouds, a new scene came into view. The earth had been plowed for planting, and the sun was shining on the fields, some plowed in one direction and some in another. It made the earth appear like a great giant checkerboard. We came down and down and then, when within a few hundred feet of the ground, I saw a man laboring in the field, his hands fixed to a plow drawn by a horse. My thoughts turned to that closing verse in the ninth chapter of Luke in which the Master said:

"No man, having put his hand to the plough, and looking back, is fit for the kingdom of God." (Luke 9:62.)

Christ made this statement as he traveled to Jerusalem. Three men had expressed their willingness to follow him and become his disciples. The first of these said to him: "Lord, I will follow thee withersoever thou goest.

"And Jesus said unto him, Foxes have holes, and birds of the air have nests; but the Son of man hath not where to lay his head." (Luke 9:57-58)

In his teachings the Master used homely figures of speech, those having familiar, everyday character. The words "his hand to the plough" unfold a picture before us with which we are all familiar—a strong man with sinewy arms and firm step, guiding the blade straight and true, his eyes intent upon the plough, looking ahead to the furrow to be cut. Hour after hour he toils, never looking backward except to see that the furrow is straight.

Whatever the past may have been in our individual lives, it is gone. The future lies ahead, and we must face it with resolution. There is always a point from which we can begin. Even though we may have been faithful in the past, if we turn away, that faithfulness will profit us nothing. "No man, having put his hand to the plough, and looking back, is fit for the kingdom of God."

There is danger in looking backward. One must keep his eyes ahead in order to cut a straight furrow. When the plowman commences to look backward, he cuts a crooked furrow, and his work is spoiled. We cannot continue to walk forward when at the same time we are looking backward.

It makes no difference what object or occasion causes us to look backward, the backward glance commences the backward turning and may be the beginning of our disendowment in the kingdom of God.

As plowing requires an eye intent on the furrow to be made and is marred when one looks backward, so will they come short of exaltation who prosecute the work of God with a distracted attention or a divided heart. We may not see clearly the end of the furrow, but we dare not look back. Eternity stretches on ahead, challenging us to be faithful.

Conference Report, April 1961, pp. 16-18.

The Learning Process Lies Within

Over fifty years ago a wealthy captain of industry was approached by representatives of Harvard University for a substantial contribution in cash to help establish and build a graduate school of business. At first this prominent industrial leader hesitated to contribute, until he was persuaded in his own mind of the worth and importance of this educational enterprise. Once convinced, he contributed many times more than what was initially requested of him.

As they were preparing for the dedicatory services they asked this great benefactor to make a speech. He declined. They tried to prevail, but again he declined. When the dedicatory services were being held, they again persisted and asked him if he would say but a few words on this important occasion. He stood before the assembly and essentially said, "I have but one thing I would like to say to you today, to the leaders and faculty and to the students of this business school." Then after a long pause he said, "The learning process lies within."

In these five words, "The learning process lies within," is contained a wise and profound truth—a truth that to my understanding has helped shape the objectives and the methods of that great school of business for over a half century.

"The Law of the Harvest," BYU Speeches of the Year, March 6, 1966, p. 2.

It All Started From a Prayer That Night

Several years ago a young man came to my home to be interviewed for a temple recommend. He told me of the lovely girl who had consented to be his bride. I knew his parents were not members of the Church, and this fact led to our conversation. I asked him what had come about in his life to cause him to be interested in the Church and to influence him to accept the gospel and live its precepts. This is the story he told me.

Five years before this night we sat together, a little thing happened in his life—a simple thing, yet so extraordinary that it changed his course. He had been serving in the armed services and had been sent to a university in the East for some specialized training, along with two other young men.

The three of them traveled together on the flight which took them to their destination, and on their arrival they went through the procedure of registration and then were assigned to quarters. They were to room together.

He said that during the time they had traveled neither of these companions smoked, and he did not smoke because of his respect for them.

After the three became acquainted with their new quarters they drew straws for beds and then unpacked their cases. Although they were not well acquainted, they spent the evening chatting about their ambitions and their goals in life.

It was past the hour for a reasonable bedtime, and all evening he had been suppressing the desire for a cigarette. He finally suggested that they go to bed. The other two looked at each other, and then one of them said, "Shall we have prayer together before we go to bed?" Then to the other he added, "Will you speak for us tonight?" The two of them dropped to their knees, just as though they had done this all of their lives.

He said to me, "I was somewhat bewildered, but I followed their pattern and got on my knees." And as he did so, some strange fear came over him. He said to me, "I had never prayed in my life, but as this young man spoke to the Lord some warm feeling came over me—a feeling I had never experienced before."

They were soon on their feet, shook hands, and said good night to each other. In a few minutes they were in bed and the lights were out, but sleep did not come to this young man. Something had happened to him while he was on his knees, and he determined to find out what made these two young men different from other men he had known.

We never fully know how our actions and our conduct affect others. We can only try to understand by our reactions to the conduct of other people. Impropriety, looseness of morals, want of principle, vice, crime, off-colored stories, or evil doing never lift our thoughts or give us a good feeling. On the other hand, it is refreshing and invigorating to be with one who has moral rectitude, integrity, virtue, and is an example for good.

I once read these words: Example has more followers than reason. We unconsciously imitate what pleases us, and approximate to the characters we most admire. (Bovee)

The power of example is demonstrated to us when we see the results of the contagion it creates. Benjamin Franklin said, "None preaches better than the ant, and she says nothing."

These three servicemen went to school the next day and because of their heavy assignments, spent the evening in quiet study, followed by the chitchat that preceded bedtime. Then it happened again—the same thing that had happened the night before. On this occasion the one who offered the words of thanksgiving and petitioned for the blessings of the Lord was the other of the two.

As the lights went out, one of them said to my friend, "It'll be your turn tomorrow night." For the second night sleep did not come quickly. The thoughts of the words which had been spoken puzzled him for some little time, and he wondered if he would ever be able to express himself on his knees as had been done by the other two.

The next day in the classroom the assignment of that evening kept coming back to his mind. He had the same feeling he had had on many occasions in track meets when he was toeing the line in that tense moment just before the gun that challenged every ounce of strength.

He wondered about this fear that had come over him. In high school he had been a student, body officer. For two years he had been a member of the debating team. Public speaking was not new to him, but this was different.

That evening, dinner was over and the three were studying, but it was difficult for him to keep his mind on the subject. He kept thinking of those few moments that would end the day. Then it came. All the courage he had mustered that day seemed to disappear from him and he said to the other two, "I guess I don't have much religion. One of you had better do this."

One of these young men, who had seen the same thing happen so many times during the two years prior to his military service, said to him, "Prayer is just a matter of thanking your Heavenly Father for the blessings you have received and asking him for the blessings you desire. It is just that simple."

With this encouragement he got on his knees and prayed for the first time in his whole life.

For the next few weeks, every third night he took his turn and expressed appreciation for the things that the Lord had given to them and asked for that which they desired.

Then he went with the other two young men to the branch of the Church in the mission where they were attending school. Finally a period was set aside each night for a little discussion in which they taught him the gospel.

Then came the decision and the day he described as the greatest day of his life. One of these young men baptized him and the other confirmed him a member of the Church.

They were soon separated after this brief time in school. He finished his military training, filled a mission for two years, and then met this lovely girl who was now to become his companion for eternity.

It all started from a prayer that night. Prayer has changed many lives. It has had an effect on our lives, both yours and mine. Prayer is that which brings us in close communion with God.

BYU Speeches of the Year, "Pray Always," October 15, 1963, pp. 2-4.

SPENCER W. KIMBALL

Spencer Woolley Kimball became the twelfth president of The Church of Jesus Christ of Latter-day Saints on December 20, 1973.

President Kimball was born in Salt Lake City on March 28, 1895 to Andrew and Olive Woolley Kimball. When he was young, his father was sent by the First Presidency of the Church to preside over the St. Joseph Stake in Thatcher, Arizona.

President Kimball served as a full-time missionary in the Central States Mission. Upon his return from his mission, he met Camilla Eyring, and they were married in November 1917. They are the parents of three sons and a daughter.

Elder Kimball was ordained to the Quorum of the Twelve Apostles on October 7, 1943. As an apostle, he visited missions and missionaries in all parts of the world, having interviewed tens of thousands of missionaries. As president of the Church, he presided over a period of significant growth.

In 1978, President Kimball received a revelation from the Lord that extended the priesthood to all worthy male members.

President Kimball passed away in Salt Lake City on November 5, 1985.

That First Tithing Receipt

When I was a little boy in Thatcher, Arizona, my father, desiring to teach his children industry, thrift, and tithing, turned over to my sister Alice and me a patch of potatoes which he had planted.

I hoed the weeds and helped to irrigate the potatoes until they were ready to dig. Then Alice and I dug and cleaned and sorted them. We took the larger ones of uniform size and put them in a box and loaded them in my little red wagon. Then, after putting on clean overalls and dress, we pulled the little red wagon with its contents to town.

We sold our merchandise to some of the neighbors, but a kindly sister who operated the hotel was our best customer. She looked them over and bought from us regularly through the season.

After selling our first load we were so happy we could hardly wait to get home to tell our parents of our success.

Father listened to us count our money—a very great amount, it seemed to us. Then father inquired: "That's capital! Now what will you do with your money?"

We thought of ice cream cones and candy and Christmas presents we could buy. Then in his characteristic and impressive way, our father said: "Now you haven't forgotten the bishop, have you? The Lord has been kind to us. The earth is his. He sent the moisture and the sunshine and all we did was to plow and plant and cultivate and harvest. One-tenth we always give back to the Lord for his work. When you have paid your tithing to the bishop, then you may use the balance as you wish."

I think I still have in my keepsakes that first tithing receipt.

Children's Friend, April 1947, p. 147.

The Breaking of Day Has Found Me on My Knees

My beloved brethren, this is the great day of my life. I have seen hands raised many times in my life, but never have they meant quite so much as they meant today when you raised your hands to sustain and support me.

I feel extremely humble in this calling that has come to me. Many people have asked me if I was surprised when it came. That, of course, is a very weak word for this experience. I was completely bewildered and shocked. I did have a premonition that this call was coming, but very brief, however. On the eighth of July, when President Clark called me I was electrified with a strong presentiment that something of this kind was going to happen. As I came home at noon, my boy was answering the telephone and he said, "Daddy, Salt Lake City is calling."

I had had many calls from Salt Lake City. They hadn't ever worried me like this one. I knew that I had no unfinished business in Salt Lake City, and the thought came over me quickly, "You're going to be called to an important position." Then I hurriedly swept it from my mind, because it seemed so unworthy and so presumptuous, and I had convinced myself that such a thing was impossible by the time that I heard President Clark's voice a thousand miles away saying: "Spencer, this is Brother Clark speaking. The brethren have just called you to fill one of the vacancies in the Quorum of the Twelve Apostles."

Like a bolt of lightning it came. I did a great deal of thinking in the brief moments that I was on the wire. There were quite a number of things said about disposing of my business, moving to headquarters, and other things to be expected of me. I couldn't repeat them all; my mind seemed to be traveling many paths all at once. I was dazed, almost numb with the shock; a picture of my life spread out before me. It seemed that I could see all of the people before me whom I had injured, or who had fancied that I had injured them, or to whom I had given offense, and all the small petty things of my life. I sensed immediately my inability and limitations and I cried back, "Not me, Brother Clark! You can't mean that!" I was virtually speechless. My heart pounded fiercely.

I recall two or three years ago, when Brother Lee was giving his maiden address as an apostle of the Lord Jesus Christ from this stand, as he told us of his experience through the night after he had been notified of his call. I think I now know something about the experience he had. I have been going through it for twelve weeks. I believe the brethren were very kind to me in announcing my appointment when they did so that I might make the necessary adjustments in my business affairs; but perhaps they were more inspired to give me the time that I needed for a long period of purification, for in those long days and weeks I did a great deal of thinking and praying and fasting and praying. There were conflicting thoughts that surged through my mind—seeming voices saying: "You can't do the work. You are not worthy. You have not the ability." And always finally came the triumphant thought: "You must do the work assigned; you must make yourself able, worthy, and qualified." And the battle raged on.

I remember reading that Jacob wrestled all night, "until the breaking of the day," for a blessing; and I want to tell you that for eighty-five nights I have gone through that experience, wrestling for a blessing. Eighty-five times, the breaking of the day has found me on my knees praying to the Lord to help me and strengthen me and make me equal to this great responsibility that has come to me. I have not sought positions nor have I been ambitious. Promotions have continued to come faster than I felt I was prepared for them.

I remember when I was called to be a counselor in the stake presidency. I was in my twenties. President Grant came down to help to bury my father, who was the former stake president, and reorganize the stake. I was the stake clerk. I recall that some of my relatives came to President Grant, unknown to me, after I had been chosen and said, "President Grant, it's a mistake to call a young man like that to a position of responsibility and make an old man of him and tie him down." Finally, after some discussion, President Grant said very calmly, but firmly, "Well, Spencer has been called to this work, and he can do as he pleases about it." And of course when the call came, I accepted it gladly, and I have received great blessings therefrom.

Conference Report, October 1943, pp. 15-16.

You Will See Him Someday as a Great Leader

Just the other day one of my brethren came into the office to talk to me intimately and confidently. After closing the door, he said, "Spencer, your father was a prophet. He made a prediction that has literally come to pass, and I want to tell you about it." He continued. "Your father talked with me at the corral one evening. I had brought a load of pumpkins for his pigs. You were just a little boy and you were sitting there, milking the cows, and singing to them as you milked. Your father turned to me and said, 'Brother, that boy, Spencer, is an exceptional boy. He always tries to mind me, whatever I ask him to do. I have dedicated him to be one of the mouthpieces of the Lord—the Lord willing. You will see him some day as a great leader. I have dedicated him to the service of God, and he will become a mighty man in the Church.'"

I say this, not in the sense of boasting, but in humility and appreciation. It came to me as a great surprise when first I heard of it the other day. I knew my father was prophetic, and some day I hope to be able to tell you some of his many prophecies which have been literally fulfilled.

Conference Report, October 1943, p. 17.

The Story of Lazarus

Today I would like to talk to you about miraculous events, those happenings that are difficult of explanation and understanding. There are two kinds of miracles. There are temporal miracles and spiritual miracles. There are the miracles which affect the body, and those which affect the soul—the one somewhat temporary, the other much more permanent. Recently a young doctor came into my office, and it seemed from his general attitude that the greatest thing in all the world was his work of relieving pain and saving bodies and lives, protecting mortal lives. And I remembered a little incident in the book which many of you have read, *The Robe*, the story of Miriam, who in her very crippled condition kept herself hidden in her room. She became sour and bitter; nothing was good; she was very selfish. And then came along the Master in the story and touched her life. He didn't heal her body, but he touched her in such a way that her bitterness changed to sweetness, her selfishness to unselfishness. And each night when the sun was setting, her friends came and carried her out to the well in the center of the village where all the villagers came together. And there with her changed life she inspired the many who came to hear her beautiful voice as she sang from an understanding, a sweet, sympathetic heart.

Then I related to this young doctor the story of Lazarus, how he had been treated by the most skillful physician that has ever graced the earth, and how that physician emphasized the transcendency of the spiritual above the physical. Word was sent to the Savior at considerable distance from Bethany, that his great friend Lazarus was very, very ill. But according to his own words he purposely delayed going to the death-bed scene two days, and then it took him a long time to get there. And he did it on purpose; he could have gone earlier and saved this man before he died. But this is what he said, "And I am glad for your sakes"—the sakes of the followers and the disciples that were with him—"And I am glad for your sakes that I was not there, to the intent that ye may believe." It was better that this one man should die perhaps that these many might get a bit of the inspirational life of Jesus and his power, and might get an insight into the gospel that he was trying to teach to them. The sickness and death of Lazarus then provided this great opportunity for him to teach faith to a large number of people.

Assembly Addresses, February 11, 1947, pp. 2-3.

Guests of the Lord

Beloved students, you are guests here—guests of the Lord, whose funds pay in large measure for your education. You are guests of the Lord, his Church, his leaders, his administration, his people. You and your parents make a smaller but necessary contribution.

In a faraway land to the south is an old man, somewhat crippled, untrained. The children, several, are ragged; their clothes are hand-me-downs, and winter or summer they trudge barefooted to a little primitive school. The home is tiny—two small rooms, one under the other with a ladder connecting. The little mother makes baskets and sells at the public market. The father makes chairs and tables out of the native jungle trees and on his calloused, leathery bare feet, walks long distances, carrying his furniture those miles to market, hopefully. The middle man or the bargaining buyer leave him very little profit from his honest labor; but because he is a faithful member of the Church, he takes his tithing to his branch president. And it finally reaches the treasury house, and part of it allocated to the Brigham Young University. And he, this dear old man, and she, this deprived little mother, and they, these gaunt little children, along with their fellow members and numerous others who are tithepayers, become host to you—the guests—and supply a goodly percentage of the wherewithal for land and buildings and equipment and instructions.

The boy working in the cornfield in India is your host for he returns his ten percent.

The rich man living in his luxury who pays his tithing is your host.

The widowed mother with several hungry children is your hostess.

The janitor of your meetinghouse is your host.

The Navajo on the desert following his little band of sheep trying to find enough grass—he is your host. His dollars are few, his tithing is meager, but his testimony of the gospel, his dreams for his children, and his love for his fellowmen and his Lord induce him to send in his little tithing. He also becomes a joint host for you.

As guests we have opportunities and responsibilities. Our rights are few. Our demands should be fewer. As guests we gratefully accept the favors of our hosts and hostesses.

Would a guest attend a banquet uninvited? Would he dress in fatigue clothes when the host had set it up as a "black tie" affair? Would he respect the host and his position? Would he say disparaging things about his host even while accepting of his hospitality? Would he declare his freedom to eat with his fingers, laugh raucously, tell malignant stories about his host?

Would he come early or stay too late? Would he take with him the host's treasures? Would he monopolize the conversation and disregard the wishes of the host? Would he ill-behave himself, ignore the wishes of the host, or defy his requests?

Would he march or riot or demand? Would he criticize—the house too small, the temperature not right, the cook ugly, the waitresses inefficient? Because other guests have been known to be unruly, would he take license therefrom? Because other guests at other houses of hospitality destroy the property of their host, lock the doors, sit in or sleep in, would these guests follow suit?

Would guests come ill-clad? uncut? unbathed? unwashed? Would a guest belittle his host or embarrass him? Would guests declare their independence, forget their opportunities or demand their supposed rights?

The greatest of all universities is our joint blessing. Let us all together keep it the pleasant oasis in the desert, where there is water and coolness when the desert sands blast in their fury.

Let us keep it an island of beauty and cleanness in an ocean of filth and destruction and disease. Let us keep it as a spring of pure cool water though surrounded by sloughs and stagnant swamps of rebellion and corruption and worldliness outside.

Let us keep it a place of peace in a world of confusion, frustration, mental aberrations, and emotional disturbances. Let us keep it a place of safety in a world of violence where laws are ignored, criminals coddled, enforcement curtailed, buildings burned, stores looted, lives endangered.

May we keep this glorious place a home of friendships and of eternal commitments; a place of study and growth and improvement; a place where ambition is kindled and faith is nurtured and confidence strengthened, and where love for God and our fellowmen reaches its highest fulfillment.

Let it continue to be a place of confidence and common admiration and understanding, with students and instructors and staff all people of confidence, affection, and serenity.

Let us not regard this as just another university—not just classrooms and professors, and students and books and laboratories.

May we enjoy the privileges and opportunities of this great institution, and profit by our rich experience here, and extend our continued gratitude to the Lord and the joint hosts and hostesses in their gracious and generous hospitality.

My beloved young folks, stand by your guns. Stay true. Live the gospel. Love the Lord, I beg of you, in the name of Jesus Christ. Amen.

Speeches of the Year, "In the World But Not of It," May 14, 1968, pp. 12-14.

LEGRAND RICHARDS

Elder LeGrand Richards devoted more than sixty years of service to the Church in positions of major responsibility, in addition to carrying on a successful real estate business much of that time.

Elder Richards is the third apostle in direct family descent. His father was President George F. Richards of the Council of the Twelve, and his grandfather, Franklin D. Richards, was a pioneer leader, apostle, and counselor to President Brigham Young.

His mother was Alice A. Robinson. He was born February 6, 1886, at Farmington, Utah.

His Church service began when he was called to serve as a missionary to the Netherlands from 1905 to 1908. He has filled four missions and presided over two of them. He served fourteen years as the Presiding Bishop of the Church and then was ordained an apostle on April 10, 1952.

He is the author of the classic doctrinal book *A Marvelous Work and a Wonder*.

He married Ina Jane Ashton May 19, 1909, in the Salt Lake Temple, and they have four daughters and two sons.

Elder Richards passed away in Salt Lake City on January 11, 1983.

Point to That Meetinghouse

We have all heard the story about Sister Mary Fielding Smith, the mother of President Joseph F. Smith, who came in from Mill Creek with a load of produce and delivered it to the old tithing office on the block east of here. The good brother in charge, knowing she was a widow and how hard it was for her to get along, hardly had the courage to let her unload that wagon at the tithing office. He said, "Take it home. You need it as much as anyone in the Church." Sister Smith said, "I can't do it. My children must know that we pay our tithing." Has she been rewarded? Her son grew up to become the prophet of the Lord to preside over this great church.

When I was the bishop of a ward and we were building a meetinghouse, a little German widow came to me one day and said: "Bishop, I haven't received my allotment for the meetinghouse."

I said, "No, sister, and you aren't going to get one. If you will just care for those little children your husband left you with, we will build the meetinghouse."

"Ah," she said, "but I must be able to point to that meetinghouse and tell my children we have done our part."

So I said, "God bless you, sister, but you will have to say what your part is then," and she gave us a substantial contribution toward that meetinghouse.

I have met her children as I have traveled about from place to place in this church and have found them active, and I want to tell you she didn't cast her bread upon the water in vain, for as the prophet of old said, "For thou shalt find it after many days."

Conference Report, October 1947, pp. 74-75.

A Natural-born Liar

Brother Ezra Taft Benson, in his beautiful address on the home, told us of the charge the Lord has laid upon the parents in Israel to teach their children faith in the living God, repentance and baptism, and the laying on of hands, and teach them to pray and to walk uprightly before the Lord in all things, with the statement that if they failed in so doing the sin would be upon the heads of the parents. I wish every father and mother in Israel realized what that meant and what it will mean when they give a reckoning for the stewardship that has been theirs to be privileged to be the parents of these chosen spirits who are permitted to come upon the earth in this day and time.

A short time ago one of the leaders in the Aaronic Priesthood in one of our stakes handed me a copy of an article that appeared in a magazine that was published by the Kiwanis Club. I want to read a few excerpts from it:

There is a general opinion that the children are bright. In my opinion there is no greater fallacy. They are so dumb that it is a wonder we ever make really useful citizens out of them.

To illustrate, the article says, "I know a fellow who has two small boys. He is a well-educated, cultured gentleman, with a lovely wife and a nice home. Those two boys have been reared with every advantage. This man takes his golf clubs and hikes out to the golf course every Sunday morning of his life, and can you imagine it, those two boys are so dumb that they can't understand why they should be made to go to Sunday School? They think they should be permitted to go fishing or swimming Sunday morning instead of going to church! Nothing their father says to them seems to convince the dumb little creatures that they should spend two hours in church on Sunday morning."

To save time, I will relate one or two more of these comments. The next one is about the father and mother who always preface their meal with a cocktail. They have a son and a daughter in high school who went to a dinner-dance, and the father found out that the children each had a cocktail before dinner. Those two kids were so dumb that when they were called on the carpet by their dad, they couldn't understand why they shouldn't drink cocktails! "I tell you, kids are dumb."

A man who occupied a prominent position in his community, when he was out in the yard and would hit his finger with a hammer or run against a wire clothesline, would make the sky blue with his profanity, and yet when his six-year-old boy called the cat a "damned cat" because it ran across the table, the father promptly spanked him and washed his mouth out with soap, but he was never able to make that dumb kid understand that it was wrong to swear.

And there was a mother who did not like to entertain company when she wasn't in the mood, and if someone would call and want to come over to visit her, she would immediately say she had house guests and couldn't receive them, or if they wanted to speak to her on the phone and she wasn't in the mood, she would turn to her little girl and say, "Tell them I am not home." Do you know that dumb little girl lies like Ananias. The mother has done all she can to break her of it, but the child is just a natural-born liar.

Conference Report, October 1947, pp. 71-72.

The Book of Mormon in the Same Cover with the Bible

When I was in the mission field in the Eastern States, into one home I went the man was not a member of the Church, and every time I would leave he would say, "I believe I have been a Mormon all my life, but did not know it," but I could not get his wife to come in and listen to me. She would go into the next room and iron. You know ironing is a quiet job. I do not need to tell you that I usually take my "loud-speaker" along with me, just in case, and I made sure she heard all I had to say.

The last visit I made there I said, "Mrs. McDonald, you would surely honor me if you would come in today and listen to me." She finally consented. I said, "You may never see me again in this world."

We had just started our discussion and in walked her son from Harvard College. She said, "My boy, you are just in time. You take this book," because I had her take the Bible to follow me, "and you show us how this man is trying to lead us astray." I took one hour and a half and I closed my Bible.

The discussion that day was on the House of Israel, the new land the Lord had promised to Joseph, the ultimate final gathering in the latter days, and the two records to be kept; and I turned to her son from Harvard and said, "You tell your mother how I am trying to lead you astray, will you please?"

He said, "Mother, this man is not trying to lead you astray, he is teaching you the truth."

Before I left she said, "Mr. Richards, even if I do not believe all you say, there is something about you I cannot help but like. Will you pray with us before you go?"

In that same city we were holding a street meeting, and the Gospel Hall people were holding a convention a short distance away. They adjourned their meeting to come and try and break up ours. I said, "You men would like to be gentlemen, wouldn't you?" As I recall, there were about sixteen ministers there that night. I said, "You give us twenty minutes to finish our meeting and then we will stay thirty minutes and listen to you." I said to the crowd, "Won't we?" There were two or three hundred there, and they indicated they would. During their thirty minutes they painted the Prophet Joseph as black as anybody could. "Why," they said, "if you would let them, the Mormons would bind the Book of Mormon in the same cover with the Bible and ask us to take it and like it."

I did not like to see that meeting close right at that point, so I stepped up to this minister and said, "You would not mind if I made an announcement before the meeting closes, would you?"

He said, "No, go ahead." So I turned to the crowd and said, "If you will come back next Tuesday night at 7:30 we will tell you why we would bind the Book of Mormon in the same cover with the Bible and ask you to take it and like it." And I said, "Bring your Bibles along with you, because you will not need them after next Tuesday night if you are not willing to accept the companion volume of scripture that Ezekiel said the Lord would bring forth, the record of Joseph, which he would join to the record of the Jews and the two should become one in his hand."

When they came that night, and the crowd was larger than the previous one, I said, "How can any of us stay the hand of God from bringing forth the record he has promised?" As I remember we sold sixteen copies of the Book of Mormon that night.

Well, I have had so many experiences that I cannot understand why we cannot plant the truth in the hearts of our people until no outside thing or movement in the world can have any influence with them. We have so much more to offer than any other church in the world.

Conference Report, October 1949, pp. 176-77.

I Decided to Trade the Dollar for Five Dollars

I was out tracting in that city one day and I had been to a particular house several times when the lady of the house said, "Mr. Richards, are you trying to make Mormons out of all of us?"

"Well," I said, "I will tell you one thing, I will never ask you to join the

Mormon Church," and that seemed to put her mind at ease. Then I said, "If I could show you where you could trade a dollar for five dollars, I would not have to ask you to do it, would I?"

After I had been home a few months I received a letter from her calling me "Brother Richards." She said, "I decided to trade the dollar for five dollars. I was baptized a member of the Church last Friday night."

I think that any elder in Israel who cannot make Mormonism look better than five to one had better get hold of the scriptures and go to work and study the gospel.

I spent an hour and a half in the study of one of the most prominent ministers in the United States. He died a few weeks ago, and at the time of his death he was chaplain of the United States Senate. While I was in his study we discussed this subject. He said, "Mr. Richards, our church does not give us any hope that there will be a continuation of the marriage tie or the family unit beyond this life, but in my heart I find stubborn objections." Then he used this illustration, and it was better than I could have given him. I have used it since, myself. He said:

"When you take the kitten away from the cat, in a few days the cat has forgotten all about the kitten, and when you take the calf away from the cow, in a few days the cow has forgotten about its calf; but when you take the child away from its mother's bosom, though she lives to be a hundred years old, she never forgets the child of her bosom. I find it difficult to believe that God created love like that to perish in the grave." But he could not tell his people that from the pulpit because he could not hold his job and teach them Mormonism.

I want to tell you that we have so much more than any other church that five to one does not begin to show it. Why do we not get into the hearts of our boys and girls and our men and women so that no power under heaven will have the power to take them away from this church?

Conference Report, October 1949, pp. 177-79.

The Angels Brought That Spirit

There are those of us who have laid away our little ones in the grave, and we had that responsibility. A little daughter was born to us over in Holland while I was president of the mission there, and we kept her until she was three and a half years old. My wife has said time and time again that she knew the angels brought that spirit to her because she felt their presence, and yet we laid her away in the grave.

If we had to feel that that was the end, we would have given anything in this world to have her back again. And then we come to this great knowledge that we have in the restoration of the gospel, that she will be ours in the eternal world and we will have the joy of seeing her grow up without sin, unto salvation.

Sometimes I have thought that probably some of these choice spirits did not need the experience here in mortality like other children, and that is why the Lord has seen fit to call them home.

We had four daughters before we had a son. We were sent to California to preside over a stake down there, and our boy went out with a member of the high council and his boys, and he lost his life in an accident. That is the greatest sorrow that ever came to us, but now we are getting up on the top of the ladder, so to speak, and we look forward, knowing that these love ties are intended by God, our Eternal Father, to endure throughout the eternities.

It takes the sting away from death to know that we are going to meet those who are so dear and sacred to us. Thank God for this knowledge! I want to see our foundation here so laid that we will be worthy to stand with our loved ones and with the sanctified and the redeemed of our Father's children.

Brothers and sisters, we are a blessed people. We are blessed in the privilege of living upon the earth when the gospel has been restored and having a knowledge of its truth. We are blessed to have a foundation upon which to build our faith, which makes every day a happy day as we associate with our loved ones.

No wonder President McKay has so often said that no success in life can compensate for failure in the home. And the nearer men and women live unto God in keeping his commandments, the greater is the love in the home and the greater appreciation of the knowledge that that love can continue throughout the eternities that are to come.

Conference Report, October 1971, pp. 85-86.

Are There Any Mormons Living Around Here?

I used to like to check up a little on us when I was a mission president. I was driving along the highway in Alabama one day, and a man was hobbling along the highway. I picked him up, and as we drove along a little way, I said, "I suppose you have no idea whom you are sitting by?"

He looked me over and said, "No."

I said, "Have you ever met a Mormon elder?"

His face lighted up, and he said, "We had two of them in our home last week, and we have one of their bibles [meaning the Book of Mormon]." Then he said, "They blessed me for my leg, and when they left I said, 'Ma, when they come back next week, let's join their church.'"

I didn't know what kind of response I would get from him!

I was driving in western Florida and stopped to get some gas for my car; to a man sitting down by one of the pumps I said, "Are there any Mormons living around here?" (I knew there were!)

He said, "There is a whole colony of them here."

I said, "What kind of people are they?"

"Oh," he said, "they are the most wonderful people. One of them is my nearest neighbor, and I never had neighbors like that family." Then he said, "You don't happen to know Jim Martin up in Magnolia, do you?"

I said, "Oh, yes, I have stayed in his home."

He said, "He's my uncle. What do you think of him?"

"Oh, he is a wonderful man."

When I was going up through the marble quarries in northern Georgia, I walked ahead with the guide. He had a whole group there that he was showing around. I said, "I suppose you have no idea whom you are walking with, have you?"

He turned and looked at me and said, "No."

And I said, "Have you ever met a Mormon missionary?"

And then he stopped and turned to the whole group and said that he had lived out in Idaho, and his nearest neighbor was a Mormon. He said, "He was the most wonderful neighbor I have ever had."

Now I could tell you many stories like that, because I like to know what people think of us when they know us.

Conference Report, October 1968, pp. 11-12.

Maybe the Lord Can Save Her, But I Cannot

Following the visit of Elder Melvin J. Ballard at Jacksonville, Florida, on December 8, 1935, one of the elders, with only thirty-five cents in his pocket, started out to return to his field of labor in South Georgia. He attempted to hitchhike on the highway without the usual success, apparently for a wise purpose. About nine o'clock in the evening he found himself still quite a distance from his field of labor, so he decided he would "tract-in" (seek entertainment) for the night.

After being unsuccessful at two homes, he called at the third and was met at the door by a minister of the gospel. He introduced himself as a Mormon missionary, whereupon he was invited in. The minister explained that he was in deep distress—that his little daughter was very sick and the doctor gave them no hope for her recovery. By this time, they had entered the living room where the family was sitting, and the doctor was at the side of the bed upon which the little girl was lying.

The minister remarked, "You believe in anointing the sick with oil, do you not?" To this the elder replied in the affirmative. He then added, "I wish you would anoint my little girl—I have prayed for her without avail," and he offered the missionary a bottle of olive oil.

The elder asked if it had been consecrated, to which the minister replied, "I am afraid I do not understand what you mean," so the elder suggested that he would use his own oil, as he had a small bottle with him, and he invited the family to kneel with him about the bed to engage in prayer before performing the sacred ordinance. They seemed rather reluctant, as though they had given up all hope. The doctor remarked, "Maybe the Lord can save her, but I cannot." The elder led in prayer and then administered to the little girl, and as he removed his hands from her head she relaxed, and the doctor immediately reached for her pulse as though he feared she was breathing her last.

For about twenty minutes, the elder sat visiting with the minister and his family, at which time the doctor again felt the girl's pulse and remarked, "There is no need of my remaining any longer—your little girl will be all right. I have seen it with my own eyes and yet I cannot believe it."

Addressing the elder, the minister said, "You were seeking a bed for the night, were you not?" And being informed by the missionary that he was, he explained that he was not prepared to accommodate him, but that he was willing to take him to the hotel and pay for his room, or he would drive him in his auto wherever he wanted to go.

He explained that his destination was sixty miles from there, but the minister was perfectly willing to take him that distance, and upon reaching his destination, the minister offered the elder ten dollars for what he had done in his home, but he refused to accept the money, explaining the instruction of the Master to the Twelve when he sent them forth: "Freely ye have received, freely give."

Conference Report, April 1936, pp. 117-18.

I Am Afraid I Can't Answer That

I should like to tell you an experience I had while laboring as a missionary in New Bedford, Massachusetts, some years ago. We were approaching the Easter Sunday, and I had a discussion with a minister of the gospel about the mission of the Redeemer of the world.

I had him explain to me the God in whom he believed. Naturally, in keeping with the ordinary orthodox Christian view, he explained how God the Father, and God the Son, and God the Holy Ghost were one God, and then he went on to indicate their works and said, in substance, that they were so large that they filled the whole universe, and so small that they could dwell in our hearts; that they were the life of the plants and flowers and everything around us.

And then I interjected this question: "What are we celebrating this week?"

And he said, "The Easter."

I said, "What does that really mean?"

"Well," he said, "it's the resurrection of Christ."

I said, "Just what do you mean by the resurrection of Christ?" Then I led him to explain. I said, "You mean that the stone was actually rolled away and that when the women came to the tomb the angels proclaimed that he was not there, that he was arisen, that the very body that was taken down from the cross and laid in that tomb had arisen?" And he admitted that that was true.

And I said that in that body he appeared to his disciples and when doubting Thomas questioned the fact that he was actually the Redeemer whom they had known, he asked Thomas to put his hand in the wound in Jesus' side and feel the prints in his hands, and see that "I am the same," for, said he, "A spirit hath not flesh and bones, as ye see me have." (See Luke 24:39.)

And to indicate further the fact that he had that same body that was laid away in the tomb, he took fish and honeycomb and ate with them. I said, "Now that was the same body that laid away in the tomb, wasn't it?" And he agreed that it was.

And then I led him on through the experience of the Savior in ministering among his disciples for forty days until in the presence of five hundred of the brethren he was carried away in the clouds of heaven, and two men dressed in white apparel stood and said, as the brethren gazed into heaven to watch him ascend, "Ye men of Galilee, why stand ye gazing up into heaven? this same Jesus, which is taken up from you into heaven, shall so come in like manner as ye have seen him go into heaven." (Acts 1:11.) And he agreed that that actually happened.

And then I said, "My friend, where is the body that Jesus took out of the tomb, if he and the father are one, and an essence everywhere present in the world? Would you say that Jesus died a second death and laid his body down again?" And he thought for a few minutes. He said, "I am afraid I can't answer that. I have never thought of it before in that way."

Conference Report, April 1953, p. 71.

The Cart Before the Horse

A few weeks ago I attended a stake conference, and the stake president told me about two visits he had made to an adult member of the Aaronic Priesthood to try to induce him to quit his tobacco so that he might receive the Melchizedek Priesthood and be prepared to go to the house of the Lord with his family; and he said he had been unsuccessful.

So I said to this stake president, "Did it ever occur to you that you might have been getting the cart before the horse, so to speak? If you would go to that man and teach him the gospel of the Lord Jesus Christ, and he would become converted, you would not need to ask him to quit his tobacco."

I think of the many, many homes into which I went in the mission field. I have in mind one now. The first night there, because we would not smoke with them, and we could not drink their coffee with them, the man said, "Well, I would never join your church." Well, we did not discuss the Word of Wisdom any more for a few weeks, until we got him a little farther along. And when we got a little farther along, we did not have to ask him to lay away his coffee; it just happened. We did not have to ask him to quit his tobacco; it went out the window the same way.

I remember one man past his eighties, who had been in the government service, walking up and down the streets and lanes in Holland for years and years of his life, and all he had for a companion and friend was his cigars. He chewed them instead of smoking them. And when he heard the gospel and became converted, he laid them away; he used to chew a little licorice root to take the place of the cigars.

I never hear of men like the one the stake president referred to but what I think—if they were only converted to the truth, they would not have to be asked to quit their tobacco. I could not help thinking the other night when we had this demonstration of missionary work, if every member of the Church could see it and hear it, and all the youth of the Church, we would not have so much transgression.

Conference Report, April 1952, p. 114.

You Just Go On, and Live Right

A few weeks ago, a young lady phoned me for an appointment; and when she came to the office, she sat there and cried for a little while, and then she said, "I guess I'm jittery."

"Well," I said, "that's all right." Then when she had composed herself, she said, "Bishop, what is there for the young people today? We have war. They are taking all the boys; it looks like another great war is ahead of us. What do we young people have to live for?"

I looked at her for a few minutes and said, "Have you ever thought of the other side of the story?"

She said, "What side?"

"Well," I said, "you remember the story of the two buckets that went down in the well; as the one came up, it said, 'This is surely a cold and dreary world. No matter how many times I come up full, I always have to go down empty.' Then the other bucket laughed and said, 'With me it is different. No matter how many times I go down empty, I always come up full.'"

I said, "Have you ever stopped to realize that of all the millions of our Father's children, you are one of the most favored? You are privileged to live in the Dispensation of the Fullness of Times that the prophets of old have looked forward to, when there is more revealed truth upon the earth than there has ever been in any other dispensation of the world's history, and when we enjoy blessings and comforts of life that kings did not enjoy a few years ago. Have you ever stopped to think of that side of the story?"

And before she left, she decided that probably it wasn't as cold and dreary a world, after all, as it might be.

I said, "You just go on, and live right, and don't you lose your courage, and don't think that life isn't worth while and isn't worth living. Whether you live or whether you die or whether you are permitted to live a long life or a short life isn't going to be the thing that is going to determine the success or failure of your life; it's how you live. And if we only live right, it will not matter whether the time is short or long; we won't have to worry much about it."

Conference Report, April 1951, pp. 39-40.

Mere Boy That I Was

Now, I would like to leave one other thought with you today. You have heard a marvelous address during this conference, by Brother Ezra Taft Benson, on missionary work.

You brethren will realize that because of the war many of our boys will be deprived of the privilege of going on missions. Some of them will feel that the years they have spent in the service will have to take the place of their missions, but we have a new generation of boys coming along, the boys of the Aaronic Priesthood of this church, and I truly hope that every bishop and every father and mother will see to it that these boys grow to manhood with a desire to fill a mission for the Church.

It is not only a great responsibility that the Lord has placed upon the Church, to see that the gospel is preached in all the world for a witness unto all nations, but the great missionary system of this church does more for the membership of the Church individually and collectively than any other activity of the Church, in my judgment.

When I was a boy, I desired with all my heart to go on a mission. I remember two returned missionaries reporting their missions in the little country town where I was reared as a boy, and as I have said many times, if they did not do unusually well that night, the Lord did something for me, because when I went home, mere boy that I was, I got down on my knees and asked the Lord to help me to be worthy to go on a mission when I was old enough. When the train finally left the station here in Salt Lake and I bade farewell to my parents, I told them it was the happiest moment of my life. There were many tears shed upon that occasion, but there were a great many more tears shed in little old Holland when I left there to return home nearly three years later.

One little mother, whose daughter came to America only a few weeks before, said, "Brother Richards, it was hard to see my daughter leave, but it is much harder to see you go." A brother old enough to be my own father knelt down and kissed my hand an affectionate goodbye. As I closed my ministry, I shed tears all the way traveling from Amsterdam to Rotterdam, as I thought of how marvelously the Lord had sustained and blessed me, and what that mission meant to me.

Conference Report, April 1945, pp. 161-62.

STERLING W. SILL

Elder Sterling W. Sill was a prominent businessman, educator, popular speaker, and prolific writer.

He was born March 31, 1903, in Layton, Utah, to Joseph A. and Marietta Welling Sill. He received his education at Utah State University and the University of Utah.

In Church activity he filled a mission in the Southern States from 1924 to 1926. He was called to serve as an Assistant to the Council of the Twelve on April 6, 1954, where he served until being sustained as a member of the First Quorum of the Seventy on October 1, 1976.

He married Doris Mary Thornley September 4, 1929, in the Salt Lake Temple. They have two sons and one daughter.

Elder Sill passed away in Salt Lake City on May 25, 1994.

I Do Not Know What God Is

To try to indicate the need that exists in the world, and in our own lives, for proper religious information, I would like to tell you of an experience. I happened to be in a large eastern city on a business assignment and, inasmuch as I was in the city over Sunday and was not convenient to my own church, I went to hear one of the great Protestant ministers of the world. After the meeting was over, I was shown through their great church edifice, and I bought a book written by the minister, which I read very carefully on the train coming home.

Three weeks later I was again in this city and again went to hear this man speak. After the service was over a large group of people lined up to shake hands with the speaker. After all of the others had gone, I introduced myself and told him how much I had enjoyed his sermons and his book, but there were some things that I could not understand and I would appreciate it if he would discuss some of them with me. He had used some phrases in reference to God such as "immerse yourself in God," or "send your roots down into God," or "fill your mind with God," and I asked him if he would explain to me his conception of God.

He was very frank to say, "I do not know what God is, and I do not know of anyone who does know. If someone could find out what God is, that would be the greatest news that had ever come into the world."

I said to him, "Would you give me your idea of what is meant by the statement in Genesis (1:27) which says that 'God created man in his own image'?"

He said, "There is one thing of which I am reasonably certain, and that is that God is not an anthropomorphic God; that is, he is the God in whose image man was created."

This great man, who is one of the most popular religious leaders in the world, does not understand God, and yet Jesus said, "this is life eternal, that they might know thee the only true God, and Jesus Christ, whom thou hast sent." (John 17:3.)

In addition, this man who has taken upon himself to minister in the name of Christ does not understand preexistence or the resurrection. He does not know the difference between the Aaronic and the Melchizedek priesthoods, nor does he understand the organization of the Church, or the use of temples, or salvation for the dead. He does not understand the necessity for divine authority and a great many other simple doctrines of Jesus that are plainly mentioned and discussed in the scriptures. Yet this man is the spiritual director of thousands of people.

I was greatly impressed by the earnestness of his declaration that to know God would be the greatest information that could ever come into the world.

Conference Report, October 1954, pp. 28-29.

You Can't Merely Snap Your Fingers

Recently a stranger called me on the telephone and asked if he and his wife might come and discuss with me a great tragedy that had occurred in their family. He explained that a speeding automobile had taken the life of their only daughter, and they asked me to try and help them understand something about the purpose of life and the meaning of death and what their relationship ought to be with each other, and where God fits into the picture, and whether or not there was any use for them to try to live on.

This great tragedy weighed upon them so oppressively that they almost seemed to be suffocating, and for three and a half hours I tried as hard as I could to help them with their problem. But there wasn't much of a foundation on which to build, and I discovered that it can be a devastating thing all of a sudden to need great faith in God and not be able to find it. It wasn't that they were rebellious or that they disbelieved in God. Their skepticism went deeper; they hadn't given him a thought one way or the other. It wasn't that they disbelieved in immortality; up to this point, they hadn't cared. Then death had stepped across their threshold and taken the best-loved personality there. And then all of a sudden, they needed great faith in God and were not able to find it.

You can't merely snap your fingers and get great faith in God, any more than you can snap your fingers and get great musical ability. Faith takes hold of us only when we take hold of it. The great psychologist, William James, said, "That which holds our attention determines our action." And one of the unfortunate things in life is that we sometimes focus our attention on the wrong things.

Conference Report, April 1959, p. 117.

A Black Walnut

As I was leaving my home a few mornings ago, I stepped on a black walnut. I carried it with me as I walked to work; and as I now hold it in my hand, I think of it as a symbol of life. This walnut has a shell-like stone. And if you could see into its inside, you would discover a great net-work of stony reinforcements. And in the labyrinths in between is a substance having a gigantic power. If you were to plant this seed in the soil under the right circumstances, heat would be developed on its inside. You might turn a blowtorch on the outside of a walnut with little effect, but when heat develops inside a person or a walnut, important things begin to happen.

In the case of the walnut, a great power is created that breaks this stony shell as though it were paper, and a little shoot is sent up on its important mission toward the sun. This walnut has within itself the ability to attract from the elements in the water, the soil, and the air all of the ingredients necessary to become a great walnut tree, with wood and foliage and blossoms and fragrance and fruit multiplying by a million times the original investment.

But God did not put his best gifts into walnuts. Every human soul was created in the image of God, and each of us was endowed with a set of the attributes and potentialities of Deity. And the greatest idea that I know of in the world is that everyone who lives the principles of the gospel of Jesus Christ will be given a far more miraculous power whereby he will be able to attract from his environment all of the elements necessary to become even as God is. May God bless our efforts toward this end, I humbly pray in the name of Jesus Christ.

Conference Report, October 1967, p. 48.

The Quicksands of His Own Mistakes

Many years ago a neighbor of mine used to say over and over again that he did not want his children to follow the Church blindly. He wanted them to do their own thinking, to stand on their own feet and break their own trails. And that is exactly what they have done. Now twenty-five years later every one of them is bogged down in the quicksands of his own mistakes.

The most successful journey is made possible when we first make sure where we want to go and then get a good set of road maps and stay right on the highway until the destination is reached. I have a relative who, when she reads a novel, always reads the last chapter first. She wants to know where she is going to come out before she gets started. That is a pretty good idea for building our lives.

Nothing could please me more than to have my children follow the Church in every detail, for I know that God has prepared the road maps, and that they lead to the most satisfactory of all destinations.

Conference Report, October 1962, p. 15.

This House Was His Wedding Present

We have heard Dr. Goodell's story of the house dishonesty built. It tells of a very wealthy man who had as a part of his household a young woman to whom the entire family was devoted. She was courted and finally married by a young building contractor.

Then this wealthy man engaged the contractor to build a house for him. He had the most famous architect draw the plans. Then laying the plans before the builder, he told him that he wanted him to construct the finest house of which he was capable. He made clear that money was not an object. He pointed out that the specifications called for only the finest materials. Everything must be of the highest quality. But the builder had a little dishonesty in his heart. Thinking to make an extra profit, he built a cheap foundation. He used low-grade lumber where he thought it would not be noticed. He adulterated the paint and slurred over the plastering. He used imitation materials for the roofing.

When the young man handed over the keys of the finished building to his wealthy benefactor, he was told that this house was his wedding present. It was not very long after the young couple moved in that the inferior foundation began to crack; the rains seeped through the roof and discolored the walls. Then throughout the rest of their lives the builder's family and himself were continually reminded of his dishonesty. What a different house he would have built if he had known that he was going to spend the rest of his life in it!

Each of us is presently building the house in which we are going to spend eternity.

Conference Report, April 1962, p. 15.

I Just Don't Want Any Signboard Telling Me Where to Go

The story is told of a father and a son riding down the highway. The son was explaining to the father what he didn't like about the Ten Commandments. He said they were negative and besides, he didn't like anyone telling him what not to do.

Soon they came to an intersection in the highway. There was one signboard telling where the left-hand road led. The father took the wrong road. This greatly disturbed the son. He couldn't understand how the father could make such a ridiculous mistake. The father admitted that he had read the signboard, but he said, "I just don't want any signboard telling me where to go."

For our benefit God has erected some signboards of right and wrong, and when we are headed toward destruction the sign is flashed, saying, "Thou shalt not." What we do from there on, however, is strictly up to us.

Conference Report, October 1963, p. 81.

The "As If" Principle

Some time ago I spent a few hours with a group of missionaries. We were discussing missionary work under the two great headings of the "message" and "the messenger." We are halfway to success when we understand the tremendous importance of the message that the gospel of Jesus Christ has again been restored to the earth with the authority to officiate in all of the principles and ordinances of the gospel having to do with the celestial kingdom. But no great message is ever delivered without a great messenger.

Inasmuch as the professional approach to any accomplishment is first to isolate the problem, I said to the missionaries, "Before I can be of much help to you, I need to know what your problems are. Will each of you tell me in one word why you're not ten times as effective as you are?"

As the answers were given, we wrote them on the blackboard. However, when we analyzed them we found that every single one of them had to do with the "messenger"; none of them was about the message. I said to them, "I'm going back to church headquarters in the morning, and

I would like to be able to report what's wrong with the message." But no one had any complaint with the message. Their only problem involved changing the messenger.

One missionary said, "I can't be a good missionary because I am not friendly."

I said, "What do you mean?"

He said, "Well, my companion loves everyone, and everyone loves him. Our contacts all gather around him, but because I am not that kind of a person I am left by myself."

I said, "Would you show me what you mean by going down this aisle and shaking hands with these people the way you ordinarily do it?"

In complying, he did his usual unimpressive job. Then I said to him, "Now, will you go down this other aisle and shake hands with these other people the way your companion does it?"

Then he squared his shoulders, got a little different look in his eye and a little different tension in his muscles, as he tried to demonstrate to me how his companion did it. He seemed to be an immediate success while following the example of his companion. I told him about the famous "As If" principle of William James. Mr. James said that if you want to have a quality, act "As If" you already had it. If you want to be friendly, act "As If" you are already friendly. How long does it take one to learn to be friendly? It takes just one-quarter of a second, just long enough to make up your mind to practice the "As If" principle. If you want to be brave, act "As If" you were already brave; don't go around telling everyone how scared and weak you are. It is the axiom of the theater that each actor should live his part.

Conference Report, October 1963, pp. 79-80.

ROBERT L. SIMPSON

Robert L. Simpson served as the first counselor in the Presiding Bishopric for many years prior to being sustained a member of the First Quorum of the Seventy.

A native of Salt Lake City, Elder Simpson spent much of his life in Southern California. He graduated from Santa Monica City College, then he worked for the Pacific Telephone Company for twenty years as a plant engineer and public relations supervisor before his call to the Presiding Bishopric.

He married Jelaire Chandler of Los Angeles, and they have three children—two boys and a girl.

Elder Simpson passed away in St. George, Utah, on April 15, 2003.

Just a Few Pennies a Day

I would like to tell you also of an experience I had down in New Zealand, going into a humble Maori home. Here we had a situation where a mother and father and twelve children were living the gospel as well as anyone I have ever seen in all my life. As they would gather around each evening to have their family devotional scripture readings and have the children participate, there was a time in the evening when the father would put a few pennies in a glass jar sitting upon the mantle. The house was lighted with candles and kerosene lamps. In this humble home this little jar was always there—just a few pennies each day. This was their family temple fund. (Imagine a family of fourteen trying to save a few pennies a day, knowing that they would have to travel thousands of miles, at least to Hawaii, in order to get to the House of the Lord to do what they wanted to do.) Then they would kneel down in prayer, and from the smallest child they would take their turns and ask Heavenly Father that they might enjoy the rich blessing of having their family sealed together in order that they might have the fullness of the gospel come into their home.

I used to sit there and literally break up inside wondering how these wonderful people would ever realize this blessing. A few pennies a day—they just could not possibly get a family of fourteen to the temple on a few pennies a day, and I did not know how they could ever do it. But they prayed in great faith, and they prayed with devotion, and they meant what they said.

If someone had told me at that time that within my lifetime there would be a temple built within sixty miles of this very home, I would have said, "I don't believe it," because I did not have the same faith these people had. I am not sure that they visualized the building of a temple in New Zealand either, but they knew that their family was going to get together and be sealed and receive the rich blessings of the gospel. I want to tell you that the Lord is mindful of these people. He was mindful of their plea, and he poured his blessings out upon this family—and this family was multiplied by many hundreds throughout the length and breadth of New Zealand. It is a wonderful thing to contemplate the great blessings of the Lord to these Polynesian people as he listens to their prayers of faith.

Speeches of the Year, "The Lord Is Mindful of His Own," April 4, 1962, pp. 8-9.

Charting a Course

Victor Hugo once commented, and I quote: "When the disposal of time is surrendered to the chance of incidents—chaos will reign." And, young people, truer words were never spoken.

Let me tell you about a missionary who felt the need for charting a course. He wanted to put a little guarantee in his charted course, so this is what he did. He wrote down for himself his major objectives for the next five years. He called it his "five-year plan." On this five-year plan, I remember, he had such entries as an honorable release from his mission (which was then just starting). He had as an objective graduating with a particular grade-point average (which was quite high, I might add). Within that five-year period he hoped to be married in the House of the Lord (and he had a pretty good idea who it was going to be). I also remember he had a notation about continuing worthily in the Church while he was achieving all of these things—worthy with regard to tithing, the Word of Wisdom, attendance at sacrament meetings, being available to his bishop, being a home teacher or whatever else might need to be done which would be compatible with his busy schedule, and doing all those things that a good Latter-day Saint should do.

Now comes the important part. Having prepared this list, he made about five or six copies, with plenty of room at the bottom for additional signatures. Then he had witnesses to these objectives that he had set; he had his parents, his mission president and wife (we were greatly honored to do this), his bishop back home, and his athletic coach (whom he respected very highly), all signed as witnesses to these commitments that he had made for himself. He was the kind of boy that would not want to disappoint those whom he loved. He would want to do these things so he would not have to say to all of us, "I failed."

I can tell you now that this young man has accomplished his goals. He is ready now to take his place in the world. He feels prepared to meet whatever comes next, and, most important of all, he has already prepared a brand-new set of goals that is going to carry him for the next five years, during the struggling days of beginning his business. And I would like to state right here that I know he will make it because he has established sound goals and has the self-discipline to pursue them effectively.

Speeches of the Year, "Organizing for Eternity," April 20, 1965, p. 4.

The Game of Life

Speaking of television, last Monday night my high school-age son persuaded me to sit down and watch the second half of a football game. I have always made it a policy that no sacrifice is too great for my boy. So we sat down and watched football. While watching this game, some facts became very apparent. In fact, it had gospel application and priesthood application.

I noticed, for example, that there were no shortcuts to the goal line. It was a hundred yards in both directions. I also noticed that the team that seemed to have had the most practice, that did the best planning, that executed their plays the best, and that had the best team attitude, was the team that made the most points.

I also noticed that when team members cooperated and helped one another, the team made the most yardage.

It was also obvious that when someone broke the rules, there was always a penalty imposed. It sounds a lot like life, doesn't it? In talking about this to my boy, he said, "Fifteen yards is nothing; but, Dad, when you ground me for three days, that is too much."

We also noticed that no one was allowed to make up his own rules as the game progressed. They all lost their free agency to do that when they agreed to join the team and play according to the established rules.

And last but not least, I noticed when it was all over, the winning team was a lot happier than the team that lost.

Now brethren, we believe that "men are, that they might have joy"; and joy can best come as we obtain victory in the game of life, played according to the only acceptable rules—those set down by our Heavenly Father.

Conference Report, October 1970, pp. 98-99.

But Daddy, I Wasn't Talking to You

As a child of God kneels to pray, that individual must believe implicitly that his prayer is being heard by him to whom the prayer is addressed. The thought that our Heavenly Father is too busy to, that our message is being recorded by celestial computers for possible future consideration, is unthinkable and inconsistent with all we have been taught by his holy prophets.

It was thrilling to listen to a father relate this story about his three-year-old youngster recently, as they knelt by the crib in the usual manner for the little fellow to say his simple bedtime prayer. Eyes closed, heads bowed, seconds passed, and there were no words spoken by the child. Just about the time Dad was going to open his eyes to check the lengthy delay, little Tommy was on his feet and climbing into bed. "How about your prayers?" asked Dad.

"I said my prayers," came the reply.

"But son, Daddy didn't hear you."

Then followed the child's classic statement: "But Daddy, I wasn't talking to you."

Even three-year-olds have personal, private matters to discuss with Heavenly Father from time to time.

Conference Report, April 1970, p. 89.

The Entire Maori Battalion

Now I have something very personal to tell you in the time remaining, and I hope that I can do it in just a few minutes. I want to tell you again that the Lord moves in mysterious ways, his wonders to perform. He protects his people and he watches out for them. He is mindful of his own.

As I was being set apart for my mission about twenty-four years ago, Brother Rulon S. Wells, then of the First Council of the Seventy, laid his hands upon my head and said, "I bless you, Brother Simpson, with a knowledge of the language of the people amongst whom you will labor," and I was grateful for this blessing. So I went to New Zealand feeling elated that I was going to learn a foreign language and that this blessing had been given to me, and no one could take it away from me.

But as I got to New Zealand I did not do very much about learning that language. After about three or four weeks had gone by with not much activity on the Maori language, I had a dream. I would like to tell you about this dream. To me it is very real.

To me it is one of the significant events of my life. In this dream I had returned home from my mission. I was getting off the boat down in Los Angeles harbor from whence I had left, and there were my bishop, my stake president, my mother and dad, and all of my friends. As I came down the gangplank of the boat they all started talking to me in Maori, every one of them—my mother, my father, my bishop—all talking in Maori, and I could not understand a word they were saying. I was so embarrassed. I was humiliated. I thought to myself, "This is terrible. How am I going to get out of it?" And I started making excuses. Right then I woke up, and I sat straight up in bed, and two thoughts came forcefully to my mind. The first message:

"You will have to do something about learning this language. The Lord has given you a blessing, but, you are going to have to do something about it yourself!"

Message number two: "You are going to need this language when you get through with your mission." These thoughts kept running through my mind all through that day. Arrangements were made and we had study time allotted each day to learn the Maori language. The Lord blessed me and I was able to bear testimony in the language after a short time.

Then, to make a long story short, the mission was finished, I came home and came into Los Angeles harbor. They were all there to meet me, but they all spoke English. Not one of them spoke Maori to me.

World War II had broken out. All of the missionaries had been called home. I thought, "Now if I am called into the Army, I am just sure that I will be sent right back down to New Zealand where I can also help President Cowley. Maybe the Lord will send me down there to help him with the mission activity between military assignments."

I went into the Air Force, and sure enough, when it came time for overseas processing, I was sent to San Francisco. All the Pacific processing was done here. I thought to myself, "Here I go right back to New Zealand." However, about two days before the ship was to sail with all of our groups consisting of several hundred men, they took out about five of us—that is all, just five—and sent us all the way back to the East Coast for shipment across the Atlantic. I thought to myself, "Well, I guess I can always preach to the Maori spirits in prison when I get on the other side!"

We joined a convoy and went across the Atlantic Ocean. I saw the Rock of Gibraltar go by, and finally the ship stopped in Egypt. We got off the ship in Egypt and we were taken to our American air base. There was a very small Air Force group in Cairo, Egypt. Of all the Air Force units throughout the world, this was one of the very smallest groups. Well, if you know anything about New Zealand, here is Cairo, Egypt, and here is New Zealand. You cannot get further away from New Zealand than Cairo, Egypt. I thought, "Well, I don't know what the Lord has in mind, but I'll just do the best I can, and I am sure that everything will work out all right."

I want to tell you young people that not more than forty-eight hours had gone by when I found that right there within the very shadows of this American air base was the entire Maori battalion—the entire Maori battalion was stationed there! This was their overseas base for processing, for all of their fighting in North Africa and Italy. For nearly two years I had the privilege of being there and meeting each Sunday with these Maori boys, bearing testimony with them in their own tongue, organizing them into small groups as they went up into the front lines in order that they might have their sacrament meetings and do the thing that they needed to do. They needed me. I needed them. I want to tell you that the Lord had a hand in writing military orders because of all of the places in this world that Air Force men were being sent, very few were sent to Cairo, Egypt. Why one of them should be selected who knew a few words of Maori and who had an abiding love for the Maori people only the Lord can answer.

BYU Speeches of the Year, "The Lord Is Mindful of His Own," April 4, 1962, pp. 9-10.

Chant of the Old Maoris

I guess I should also tell you that after I had been in New Zealand for just a short time, I went down to a place called Judea, in Tauranga. The mission president said, "I want you to go down there and learn how to speak Maori." He didn't say anything to the branch president, but the branch president had assigned all the Primary children to teach me how to speak Maori. I was helping to build a small chapel. While we were up there hammering nails, these Primary children would sit down on the grass and jabber Maori to me all day. They wouldn't speak any English. They knew how to speak English too—they knew more languages than I did. But, they wouldn't answer me if I spoke to them in English. I had to speak Maori to them. They were forcing me to learn this language, that I might be a more effective missionary.

I remember they taught me a little song. Oh, how grateful I was to them! I thought to myself as I was learning this little ditty, "Here I am, learning the great chants of the old Maoris, passed down through hundreds of years. I have just been in New Zealand a few weeks and already I can sing this old Maori war chant." I didn't know at the time what it meant, but I will never forget it as long as I live.

Imagine my surprise when I found out it was "Hey diddle diddle, the cat and the fiddle, the cow jumped over the moon!" The world is getting pretty small, and I think that is a fairly good indication.

BYU Speeches of the Year, "Do Your Standards Show?", October 19, 1963, pp. 3-4.

The Wyoming Cowboy

I am going to conclude by telling you just one more story, quickly, about a young man who was called into the mission field. He felt inadequate for the call—his grammar was poor, he did not know how to talk to people, and he felt that he could not carry out his mission. The reason he had this inferiority complex was because he had to quit school when he was 15 years of age because his father passed away. This boy became the family breadwinner—he had to take over the ranch in Wyoming. The bishop assured him, however, that his place was in the mission field now that he was nineteen.

So into the mission field he traveled, halfway around the world, and there on his very first day he was told that Sister Johnson was having the missionaries for dinner, which was the custom of that mission. On the first day they went to her home and tasted the food of that land and learned something of the customs. Sister Johnson's husband was not a member of the Church. He knew the scriptures very well—he knew everything that a Mormon missionary did not know on his first day in the mission field. After dinner he would get these missionaries in a corner. He would try to embarrass them, and he found great delight in doing so. More often than not the missionaries went home determined that was not going to happen to them again, so they set their alarm clocks up thirty minutes earlier in order that they might get some extra studying in.

But here comes our young cowboy from Wyoming, feeling inadequate in his calling. Mr. Johnson was in the corner with him after dinner, and the missionary was embarrassed until tears came to his eyes. The thought came into his heart, "I will go to my mission president in the morning and tell him that I must be released. I have come into the mission field unprepared." Just then something lifted him right out of his chair, and he stood up to his full six-foot four-inches of Wyoming cowboy. He reached over and took Mr. Johnson by the shoulders, and he pulled him in real close. He said, "Now, Mr. Johnson, I do not know how to argue these things with you. I do not know how to debate with you. I have not had a lot of schooling, but I know why I have to come halfway around the world. If you will just stand here for four or five minutes, I am going to tell you about it." Mr. Johnson had no choice. The young elder from Wyoming then had a captive audience. Then, for the next five or six minutes, this young cowboy from Wyoming told the man the Joseph Smith story—the story that rang true in his heart. He had been taught the story at the knee of his mother. He used to read the story as he rode the range. He loved it and he knew that it was true, and so he told it to Mr. Johnson with all of the sincerity of his heart. After five or six minutes had gone by, there were tears in other eyes.

To make a long story short, there was a baptism about four or five weeks later. I think you know who was baptized and who did the baptizing. Mr. Johnson had heard the Joseph Smith story from every missionary who had ever been in his home—some who had been all of the way through college, some who had their gifts developed; but never had he heard it with the gift of the Spirit of God like he heard it from the unschooled lips of a cowboy from Wyoming on that wonderful day. He was listening to something beyond the words that were traveling from lip to ear. There was something from the heart of this young missionary into his heart-bearing witness to him, "This young man is telling me the truth. Poorly as he is telling it, poor as his grammar is, I know that it is true because God is revealing it to me." And he joined this great church.

BYU Speeches of the Year, "Gifts of the Spirit," October 18, 1966, pp. 9-11.

From the Mission Office

Someone has properly observed that it doesn't take money to pay tithing—it takes faith.

In this respect, I shall always remember the faith of an old Maori brother in New Zealand. As the missionaries came to his humble little fishing shack located well off the beaten track, he hurried to find an envelope that contained a letter addressed to him and in which he had also stuffed a sizable sum of hard-earned money. He promptly handed the envelope containing the money and letter to the missionaries. This fine brother didn't have the ability to read the letter when it arrived, for it was written in English and his tongue was Maori, but he could read the financial figures contained in it, and he recognized the letter-head as being from the mission office. He thought the mission needed the cash amount mentioned for some special purpose, and he had it all ready for the missionaries.

After translating the letter for him, it was now clear that the letter merely confirmed his annual tithing settlement and stated the total amount paid for the previous year. His faith was such that he stood ready to pay the same amount all over again if the Lord's servants needed it for the work.

Conference Report, April 9, 1966, p. 52.

ELDRED G. SMITH

Elder Eldred C. Smith was the seventh Patriarch to The Church of Jesus Christ of Latter-day Saints and is the great-great-great-grandson of Joseph Smith, Sr., first Patriarch to the Church and who is the father of Joseph Smith, Jr., founder of the Church.

Elder Smith was born January 9, 1907, in Lehi, Utah, son of Hyrum C. and Martha Gee Smith. When his father became presiding Patriarch to the Church (this is the only office in the Church that follows the patriarchal line from father to son), the family moved to Salt Lake City, where young Eldred was educated in public schools and the University of Utah.

His first call to Church service was as a missionary to the Swiss-German Mission from 1926 to 1929.

He was sustained Patriarch to the Church on April 6, 1947, and traveled throughout the stakes of the Church as one of the General Authorities. He has given thousands of patriarchal blessings.

He married Jeanne Ness August 17, 1932, in the Salt Lake Temple. They have two sons and three daughters.

Elder Smith was named an emeritus General Authority on October 6, 1979.

What a Patriarchal Blessing Can Do

An example of what a patriarchal blessing can do came to me in a story which I have repeated many times, which a woman told me. As a young woman she lived in a small town. When she finished high school, there was no further opportunity to continue her education. There was no further opportunity to get work so that she could be independent, so she came to Salt Lake City where she found herself a job. As time came for registration at the University, she became very anxious to go to school again, and knowing that there was not a possibility, under present conditions, she felt quite disheartened. She went to the patriarch and received her patriarchal blessing, and in the blessing he promised her that she should receive a good education.

She was elated, and she went out of the office feeling very happy. Before she had gone half a block, she said, she fell to earth out of her cloud with a realization that going to college cost money, and she did not have any, nor the means to get it.

The opportunity and possibility of going to college at present did not seem to be at all possible, which made her very downhearted again. And the thought came to her to go visit her aunt, who was living in Salt Lake City. Without stopping to analyze that impression she turned, and instead of going back to work she went to visit her aunt and told her aunt of her experience, crying on her shoulder. And her aunt said to her, "I know an elderly woman who lives down the street a few blocks. She has at various times helped young girls get through college in return for the help the girls can give to her. I do not know whether she has help now or not, but," she said, "this woman knows who I am. Go down and see her and tell her I sent you."

She went on the run to this elderly woman's home, and within two weeks from the time she received her patriarchal blessing, she registered at the University of Utah, signed a promissory note to pay for her education, and eventually paid for it. She said if she had stopped to question the first impression she got to go visit her aunt, she would have said to herself, "Why should I go visit my aunt and tell her my troubles? I came to Salt Lake City to be independent; why not be independent? She cannot help me with my troubles; she has enough of her own. She doesn't have space in her home to let me sleep there, let alone board me or help me. Why need I go and bother my aunt?" But she did not stop to analyze that impression; she acted on it. As a result she met the woman who gave her the opportunity of receiving her education.

Conference Report, April 1952, pp. 39-40.

I Met the Challenge

Live the gospel first, then teach it to others. Declare your testimony to others on every occasion. There is a power in bearing your testimony.

I remember an occasion in the mission field in Germany, when I had been tracting. I was getting a bit discouraged, having met nothing but passive attention. After climbing some stairs I knocked on a door, and a large man opened it and with a very gruff attitude greeted me. I gave him my brief message, as we did in those days in presenting a tract at the door. He turned and picked up a handful of leaflets off the table near the door, and shook them in my face, and declared to me that I was the fifth person who had been to his door that day with just such leaflets. He was a large man and very rough in his approach. I expected any moment that I might be thrown down the stairs, but he declared that none of us knew that we had the gospel. He said, "You all say that it is true, this is the way; you all say that. None of you know."

I met the challenge, and I stood straight before him and looked him square in the eyes. And I bore my testimony to him that I knew that this is the gospel of Jesus Christ and the only method by which he could gain salvation, and I went on at some length bearing my testimony to this man. Afterward I was surprised at the fluency of my speech because I had not been in Germany very long. I did not understand the language very well, but when I had finished, he had changed his tone and very humbly begged my pardon and promised to read the tract, which I am sure he did.

Conference Report, October 1951, pp. 81-82.

The Only Ones Sitting in the Audience

I have heard President Clark a number of times refer to his theme song, as he calls it, that of unity; and with his permission I would like to join his chorus. We should all join his chorus, not only in words, but in action. Paul taught the same doctrine when he wrote to the Ephesians:

"I therefore . . . beseech you that ye walk worthy of the vocation wherewith ye are called,

"With all lowliness and meekness, with longsuffering, forbearing one another in love;

"Endeavoring to keep the unity of the Spirit in the bond of peace.

"There is one body, and one Spirit, even as ye are called in one hope of your calling;

"One Lord, one faith, one baptism,

"One God and Father of all, who is above all, and through all, and in you all." (Eph. 4:1-6.)

When I talk about unity in the gospel, I am often reminded of an experience that I had while on a mission in Germany. When this German choir sang to us yesterday in the conference meetings, I was reminded again of those experiences, especially when I was assigned to work in Celle in the Hannover District in Germany. Once a month we went to the little town of Uelzen, which was a self-sustaining branch. We went there to get their reports and to help them as we could. My companion was assigned to the branch the same time I was, so this first visit to Uelzen was a new experience for both of us.

We took our seats in the first meeting we attended in the front of the hall. The branch president announced that the meeting would be started by the choir singing such and such a song. I looked about and found no choir up in front, but before I could ask any questions or discover an answer to the problem in my mind as to where the choir was coming from, my companion and I found ourselves the only ones sitting in the audience. The entire congregation, except for my companion and I, had gone up to the front and sang as a choir. It is no wonder we have Saints who can come here and produce a chorus such as we had yesterday.

I found from the reports that they not only all sang together, but they worked together. I found that there was 100 percent membership of the branch paying 100 percent tithing—and that was not just the month that I went there on that one visit, but that was the report I got all the time I was there. Attendance in their meetings was the same. They worked together in everything they did. I discovered also that there were two women in the branch at that time whose husbands had gone to America, and that the branch had agreed together, before these two men left, that they would all work together. They would keep the commandments of the Lord to the best of their ability; they would do all that was required of them without excuse; nothing would stop them from fulfilling the responsibilities given to them. Those who remained in the branch would see to it that the wives of these two men were taken care of, that they would not be in need.

The two men who left for America agreed that they would do likewise in living the commandments of the Lord, and that they would find jobs and work hard and save their money and send for their wives as soon as possible. It was not long until I was transferred from that section of Germany, and then soon after, I was released to come home.

Some twenty years later, after I became the Patriarch to the Church, I had an appointment to give a blessing to a young girl. When she arrived, her mother was with her. I found that the mother was one of those two sisters whose husbands had left Uelzen when I was over there. I had a long talk with this sister and her daughter. The daughter, of course, had grown up from a small child, and her mother told me this story: that one by one, or two at a time, as occasion came, different members of the branch would have the opportunity of leaving and coming to America, until finally, before World War II broke out, there was not one member of the Church left in that branch in Uelzen. They had all come to America safely before the war broke out.

Then she told me also that in the end of the war, when the American soldiers invaded that section of Germany, for some reason unknown to her, the German soldiers set up a resistance in Uelzen which resulted in a four-day battle. The bombings and general destruction were such that there was not a house left in the section where most of the Saints had lived, yet there was not a member of the Church left in Uelzen—a result and reward of unity, working together to keep the commandments of the Lord.

This is a challenge to us, brothers and sisters, that we might do as they did in Uelzen—that we might live the commandments of the Lord as they did.

Conference Report, October 1955, pp. 62-63.

This Is Priesthood Order

In the beginning, God said: "It is not good for man to be alone."

One of the fundamental purposes of this life is to have experiences whereby we may learn to be perfect. Man is not perfect without the woman, nor is the woman perfect without the man.

Priesthood and motherhood go hand in hand. Neither is complete without the other. Both are eternal. A perfect family requires the proper fulfillment of both. This life is to help us fulfill these two responsibilities, that we may exercise them through eternity.

Priesthood is patriarchal, which means "of the fathers." A married man is the patriarch of his home and is responsible to bless members of his family. The exercising of this privilege could be a means of preventing many broken homes. We think of a priesthood holder as one who should bless his children, baptize and confirm them, and perform the other ordinances of the gospel in behalf of members of his family. His responsibility is not only to bless his children, but his wife is an important member of his family too. Yes, we think of blessing the wife when she is sick, but if the relationship between husband and wife becomes a bit strained, wouldn't it be a good thing for the husband to give his wife a blessing for the purpose of increasing the unity and love for each other?

I remember an experience I had when a good sister who wanted a special blessing came to my office. When I asked her why she wanted a special blessing, she refused to tell me. I learned from her that her husband was a member of the Church and held the Melchizedek Priesthood, so I spent considerable time trying to teach her the principle of priesthood order, where the father in the home should bless the members of the family, and concluded a long discussion of teaching her this principle by having her go home to get her blessing from her husband instead of from me.

Sometime later she returned to my office, refreshed my memory of this experience, and said she left my office very resentful. Here I thought I had done a good job in teaching her this principle of priesthood order, so I had to ask more questions to find out what had happened.

She said the reason she refused to tell me why she wanted a blessing was that she wanted the blessing because there wasn't the proper relationship between her and her husband, and then I had sent her home to get a blessing from her husband. So naturally she was a little bit resentful.

Then she added, "That was one of the finest things that ever happened." She said she went home, she prayed about it, she thought about it, and then finally she mustered enough courage to ask her husband for the blessing. Of course it shocked him, but she was patient; she let him think it over a bit, ponder about it, and pray about it; and finally he gave her a blessing. Then she added, "There has never been such a fine relationship in our home in all our lives as we have had since he gave me that blessing."

I could see what had happened. This is a two-way street. First, she had to clean her side of the slate and humble herself. Then she asked him for the blessing, and he had to humble himself and clean his side of the slate. Then he sealed the blessing upon her which they had fulfilled by living the law upon which the blessing was predicated. This is priesthood order.

Conference Report, April 1965, pp. 114-15.

Bishop, I See What You Came Here to Tell Me

I am reminded of the story which is so often told, and which you all know, of the bishop who visited a member who had become inactive in the ward. They sat in front of an open fire in the fireplace in silence. And the bishop, presumably thinking about how he could approach the subject, reached forth with the tongs and lifted a hot, live coal from the fire and set it on the hearth in front of the fire. They sat in silence and watched the hot, live coal gradually turn cold and black and lifeless. Then the bishop picked up the coal again with the tongs, and set it back into the fire with the other living coals, and watched it again regain its life and its fire and its heat and its warmth. Still nothing was said. Finally the man said, "Bishop, I see what you came here to tell me."

Through meeting together the fire of our testimony is kept alive and glowing. It is through meeting and working together that we grow in faith and in knowledge. When we withdraw from Church activity we become as the lone coal on the hearth, cold and lifeless.

Conference Report, April 1953, p. 29.

N. ELDON TANNER

N. Eldon Tanner served as a counselor to four presidents of the Church—David O. McKay, Joseph Fielding Smith, Harold B. Lee, and Spencer W. Kimball.

He was born in Salt Lake City, May 9, 1898, and was taken to Canada when three weeks old, where he lived continuously until his call to Salt Lake City.

He was well-known in Canada as both a business and political leader, as well as serving as a bishop and stake president before his call as an Assistant to the Twelve on October 8, 1960.

He was ordained an apostle and became a member of the Quorum of the Twelve on October 11, 1962. His service as a member of the First Presidency began in 1963.

He married Sara Isabelle Merrill of Hill Spring, Alberta, on December 20, 1919. They have five daughters.

Elder Tanner died in Salt Lake City on November 27, 1982.

You and the Rest of the World

I would like to tell you one or two experiences that I have had in my life. You know, when I was a young man my father pointed his finger at me and said, "Young man, I want you to realize that this world is divided into two great groups—you, and the rest of the world." He was serious about it, and he made me feel serious about it before we had finished talking. He said, "Regardless of what the rest of the world does, it cannot save you; and regardless of what the world does, it cannot destroy you. It is what you do yourself that determines what is going to happen, whether you are going to be loved and respected and happy and successful while you are living here, and whether or not you are going to meet your Heavenly Father the way you would like to meet him."

When I was president of the Edmonton (Alberta, Canada) Branch we had a young man there who was the only member of the Church on his high school basketball team. That young man and I were pretty close friends, though he was only a sixteen-year-old boy. He said to me, "You know, I don't know how I am going to hold up."

I said, "Listen, you have something that these boys don't have. They don't know anything about our Word of Wisdom. They don't know several things that we have in the Church. They don't know that they are spirit children of God. If I were you, I would just tell these boys something about the Word of Wisdom, and how these things may destroy your body, and how detrimental they are to you, and how they will impede your playing, and so on."

You know, he set out to do that, and he became more or less a hero with those boys. Before that year was over, there wasn't a single boy on the team who was using tobacco. Now, how easy it would have been for him to follow those boys and be one of them. You know, it is easy for anybody to be a follower, and he doesn't gain much by doing it, unless he is following the righteous.

It is a little difficult to be a leader, to take your stand. We have an individual responsibility. The world is divided into the two great groups, and remember, you are one of them. The individual is one of them, and his success depends upon his individual stand.

Conference Report, October 1968, p. 103.

I Am Going to Report to the Lord Tonight

I recall an experience while I was a deacon. I had a sister who had spinal meningitis, and a very severe case of it. We had been taught to pray. I remember so well how my father used to get us together in family prayer and how he would talk to the Lord. He just didn't say a few words and off we would go to the fields. He kneeled down with us and he talked to the Lord as one man would talk to another. He told the Lord about some of our weaknesses and some of our problems where we had failed, and he apologized for us. [He would say:] "Eldon didn't do exactly what he should have done today. We are sorry that he made this mistake. But we feel sure, Heavenly Father, that if you will forgive him, he will determine to do what is right. Let your Spirit be with him and bless him that he can be the kind of boy we would like to have."

My, that was a help! He used to say in the morning, "Let your blessings attend us as we go about our duties that we may do what is right and [we will] return tonight to make a report." I used to think of that: "I am going to report to the Lord tonight." It helped me materially in the kind of life I lived during the day....

I started to tell about my sister who had spinal meningitis, and she was very sick. I remember one night as we (the family) knelt in prayer Father said to me, "My boy, you hold the priesthood now; I wish you would lead in prayer, and remember Lillie." She had been, and was at the time, very, very sick. They didn't know whether she would live or not. I remember as I kneeled down in prayer with the family and was mouth in that prayer the feeling that came to me, and the understanding, that she would be made well. My sister began to get better from that day forward. Today she is the mother of three children and grandmother of five children; she is working and enjoying good health.

In His Footsteps Today, [Salt Lake City: Deseret Sunday School Union, 1969], pp. 82-83.

The Value of a Good Home

I well remember when I was a young lad and wanted to go to normal school to learn to be a teacher. Father couldn't really spare me, let alone finance me. But he said, "If you can arrange to borrow the money to go through school, you have my blessing."

I'll never forget going into that bank. I was frightened to death to go in there and speak to the manager of that bank and ask him if I could borrow $400. (That wouldn't get you very far today, would it?) But it gave me enough so that I thought I could get through by working on Saturdays and holidays.

The banker said, "Who are you anyway?" I said, "I'm Eldon Tanner."
He said, "Are you So-and-So's boy?"
I said, "No, I'm N. W. Tanner's boy."
"N. W. Tanner's boy?" "Yes."
"When can you pay this money back?"
I said, "I'll pay it back as rapidly as I can out of my first earnings."

He said, "If you are N. W. Tanner's son, I'm prepared to let you have the money." No security other than my father's name! I thought then, "I'm going to keep my name clean so that my credit will be good, and so that my posterity might have the benefit of an unsullied name."

BYU Speeches of the Year, "My Experience and Observations," May 17, 1966, pp. 7-8.

He Had Real Courage

Two years after this Church was organized, two missionaries of the Church were out in a rural area where there was a man by the name of John Tanner. That man heard that some missionaries from a new church were going to have a meeting in the schoolhouse. Though he was a cripple, and had been for months, and the doctors couldn't find a cure for his ailment—he was in a wheelchair—he insisted that his boys take him to hear those missionaries speak so that he could put them right—keep them in their place and see that no false doctrine was taught.

He sat right down in front of the speaker, and he heard the one missionary tell about the restoration of the gospel and the apostasy; and the other told about the Book of Mormon, that the priesthood was restored, and so on. John sat there and listened to them, and he never checked them on anything, he didn't heckle them, he didn't try to put them right.

When the meeting was over he said to his son, "I want to meet those missionaries." His son went up and got the missionaries and brought them down and introduced them to him. John said, "Would you men like to come and stay with me tonight in my home?" There he discussed the gospel with them for hours, on into the early hours of the morning. He finally said, "If I weren't a cripple, I think I would like to apply for baptism." See the change in that man that took place in less than twenty-four hours when the gospel was preached to him!

One of the missionaries said, "Do you think the Lord could heal you?"

He thought about it and said, "I think he could if he wanted to."

Then they told him that the Lord has said, "Is any sick among you? let him call for the elders of the church; and let them pray over him." (James 5:14)

They said, "We are elders and we hold the priesthood of God, which is the power of God delegated to man to act in his name. Would you like us to administer to you?"

He said, "Yes."

They administered to him, and that very day he left his wheel chair and got up and walked three-quarters of a mile to be baptized, and never went back to his wheel chair. He had real courage, and I am so thrilled to think that that great-great-grandfather of mine had the courage to join the Church and to realize that the thing that meant most in his life was the gospel plan of life and salvation. Because he lived up to the teachings of the gospel, and his son, and his son, and his son (who was my father) did the same thing, I am here today. The most important thing in the lives of any one of those men was the gospel of Jesus Christ and living its teachings.

BYU Speeches of the Year, "My Experiences and Observations," May 17, 1966, pp. 6-7.

HENRY D. TAYLOR

Henry D. Taylor was born in Provo, Utah, on November 22, 1903, the son of Arthur N. and Maria Dixon Taylor.

He graduated from Brigham Young University in 1929 and in 1960 was presented the Alumni Distinguished Service Award from that school. He earned a master's degree from the New York University School of Retailing in 1937. He then embarked on a career as a prominent business executive in Provo, Utah, before his call as an Assistant to the Quorum of the Twelve on April 6, 1958. He was later sustained as a member of the First Quorum of the Seventy on October 1, 1976.

He married Alta Hansen of Richfield, Utah, in the Salt Lake Temple on December 26, 1929. She died on July 6, 1967. On September 9, 1968, he married Ethelyn Peterson Taylor.

Elder Taylor passed away in Salt Lake City on February 24, 1987.

We Love One Another

A lonely young Persian student was in Munich, Germany, struggling to find a meaning to life. He was deeply disturbed by the materialism and selfishness that seemed to fill the world, and especially postwar Europe. He heard a knock at the door, and two humble Mormon elders stood before him. He was not the least interested in religion. In fact, cynicism and doubt had filled his soul until he was very nearly persuaded that there was no God nor any real meaning to life. The only thing that interested him about these two young men was their English accent. He had mastered four languages, but English was not one of them.

He invited them in, but as they started their discussion, he cautioned: "I don't want to hear about your God, nor do I want to hear about how your religion got started. I only want to know one thing: what do you people do for one another?" He waited, and a look of doubt crossed his dark features, as the elders exchanged glances.

Finally, the spokesman for the two said softly, "We love one another."

Nothing he could have said would have been more electrifying than this simple utterance had upon this young Persian, for the Holy Ghost immediately bore testimony to his soul that these missionaries were true servants of the Lord. Shortly thereafter he was baptized, and he presently is in this country receiving his doctorate degree at a local university—all because a young Mormon missionary declared a simple truth, "We love one another."

Conference Report, April 1969, p. 37.

Armchair Generals

While World War I was raging in Europe, there were certain individuals here at home who would sit back in their easy armchairs, surround themselves with maps, and follow the progress of battle by reading the newspapers. They were extremely critical of the generals and those who were directing the campaigns and were very eager and vocal in outlining the strategy they would employ if in similar positions of leadership. These individuals were referred to as "armchair generals."

Prior to demolition of old buildings or the construction of new buildings, a solid fence is built to protect passers-by. It has become a practice to bore holes in the fence or to install glass portholes. From these observation points many pause and watch with interest the demolition or construction activities. There are those among the viewers who would improve the way the job is run. Some would knock a building down immediately, while others would have it done bit by bit. Then there are those who would make changes in the architectural design of the building. Others are critical of the manner in which the cement is poured, the bricks are laid, and the glass is installed. These persons are known as "sidewalk superintendents."

Then there is another group belonging to this category. While riding in a car they are continually offering suggestions to the driver as to how the car should be operated, the speed that should be traveled, when to turn, and the signals to be employed. These are the "back seat drivers."

The Church becomes an object of criticism from just such "experts." They are dissatisfied with the manner in which the superintendent manages the Sunday School. They find fault with the way the bishop conducts the affairs of the ward. The stake president does not please them, and they criticize his administration. They are unhappy with the way the tithing is disbursed. These are the persons who find no fault with their own actions, but seem willing and anxious to confess another person's sins.

The Savior was chastising such groups as these when he said, "And why beholdest thou the mote that is within thy brother's eye, but considereth not the beam that is within thine own eye? . . . thou hypocrite, first cast out the beam out of thine own eye; and then shalt thou see clearly to cast out the mote out of thy brother's eye." (Matthew 7:3-5.)

I believe that is the same thought that the poet Burns desired to express when he penned the lines:

O was some Power the giftie gie us
To see Oursels as ithers see us!
—Robert Burns, "To a Louse"

I assure you that I am not against criticism, if it is the right kind. Constructive criticism can be good and helpful. Destructive criticism can be bad and harmful. Many years ago my mission president gave this sound advice: "If criticism is just and given kindly, accept it and give thanks for it. If it is just and given unkindly, accept it. But if it is unjust and given unkindly, pay no heed to it."

A critical attitude and faultfinding with the Church, if persisted in, can easily lead to apostasy. A good motto to adopt and follow is, "If you can't improve on silence, say nothing."

Conference Report, October 1960, pp. 8-9.

Look at That Big Tree

A boy was extended an invitation to visit his uncle, who was a lumberjack up in the Northwest. For months the boy had looked forward with anticipation to this trip as an exciting adventure. Finally the time came for his journey to the vast timber empire of our country. His uncle met him at the depot, and as the two pursued their way to the lumber camp, the boy was impressed by the enormous size of the trees on every hand. There was a gigantic tree that he observed standing all alone on the top of a small hill. The boy, full of awe, called out excitedly, "Uncle George, look at that big tree! It will make a lot of good lumber, won't it?"

Uncle George slowly shook his head, then replied, "No, son, that tree will not make a lot of good lumber. It might make a lot of lumber but not a lot of good lumber. When a tree grows off by itself, too many branches grow on it. Those branches come from trees that grow together in groves. The trees also grow taller and straighter when they grow together."

It is so with people. We become better individuals, more useful timber when we grow together rather than alone.

This growing together places a responsibility upon each one of us. We should try fully to appreciate all our associates, help them, love them, teach them the gospel of the Lord Jesus Christ, his plan of salvation for them. We are all the children of God. We can help others; they can help us. Together we can become valuable timber in effectively building his church in which we are blessed to hold membership.

Somewhere out there in the wards and branches and cities where you live are those who are lonely—lonely for want of the light of truth; lonely for the association of those who reflect the Spirit of the Master; lonely, though they may not realize it now, to be a part of the body of Saints that make up the kingdom of God here on the earth. Don't let them stand alone in the dark. Go to them. Let your life be a lamp to their feet. Guide them till they stand with you and your associates in the gospel of our Redeemer.

This is your responsibility, your obligation, your mission, your privilege. May you fulfill all of those opportunities humbly and nobly, I pray in the name of the Lord Jesus Christ.

Conference Report, April 1965, pp. 54-55.

Excess Baggage

Rather recently I enjoyed my first experience of traveling on a jet-propelled plane. It was amazing the speed at which we traveled. Less than two hours after leaving Denver, we were in Chicago. Prior to departure we were required to place our luggage on a pair of scales. If the weight was under forty pounds, the amount allowed each passenger, a green light flashed. But if the weight exceeded forty pounds, a red light flashed and a bell rang. The weight exceeding the allowance is considered excess baggage and a penalty or additional charge is levied. When the red light flashes, one begins to consider the unnecessary articles he could have left behind, such as an extra pair of shoes, for example.

The thought occurred to me that this earth life is also a rapid flight or journey. We are traveling toward a desirable destination, that of eternal life and exaltation. Now the Lord has said, "For behold, this is my work and my glory—to bring to pass the immortality and eternal life of man." (Moses 1:39.)

Our goal should be to become perfect, even as our Father in heaven is perfect. It would be well in early life to select and make secure the characteristics and traits needed for this journey of life, discarding the ones which are harmful and which might be classed as excess baggage. We can then be sure, as we continue our journey, that the green light and not the red one will be flashing.

What are some of the traits that might be regarded as excess baggage on our journey toward perfection? To mention but a few: hate and anger and the holding of grudges, a hot temper and a quick tongue, envy, jealousy, and greed, a critical attitude resulting in faultfinding, backbiting, and judging harshly. All these are excess baggage, and we shall have to pay dearly for them.

In contrast there are certain basic, essential characteristics or traits that are very desirable. They constitute legitimate or necessary baggage on our life's journey. One is love, love for our Father in heaven, love for fellowmen and neighbors. The Savior taught, "But I say unto you, Love your enemies, bless them that curse you, do good to them that hate you, and pray for them which despitefully use you, and persecute you. (Matt. 5:44.)

Someone has said, "Be kind to your enemies, for you are the one who made them."

Conference Report. April 1960, p. 119.

He Received His First Paycheck

It is pleasing to the Lord that the poor and needy be provided for. Running like a golden thread through the scriptures, which contain the word of the Lord, comes a message loud and clear: "Thou shalt remember the poor and the needy."

The Lord has affirmed and reaffirmed that it is his purpose to see that they are cared for, but he has made it equally plain and clear that it must be done in the way and manner that he will indicate or prescribe.

In spite of the Lord's concern for the well-being of the needy, he has pointed out and proclaimed emphatically that they themselves have a responsibility, and if they find it necessary to seek assistance from the Church, they are under obligation to work to the extent of their physical ability for that assistance. Idleness has been designated by the Lord as being a curse, and to receive without giving is contrary to his desires. The beautiful and vital principle of work removes the welfare program from the category of a dole, which has been denounced as an evil. To re-enthrone work and make it a ruling principle in the lives of the Church members is one of the primary purposes of the welfare program.

A man over thirty years of age had never been able to work, due to cerebral palsy, from which he had suffered since birth. He was brought by his bishop to a Deseret Industries plant, where someone with love and kindness patiently taught him to cut the buttons from old clothes that were brought daily into the Deseret Industries plant. This became something he could do, and fairly skillfully too. For the first time in his life this man felt he was a useful member of society. With joy and pride he turned each day to his humble task. And then came the day that he received his first paycheck. With trembling, uncontrolled movements he took the check, read the amount eagerly, and proudly placed it in his wallet as he had seen others do, but which he had never been able to do in all his thirty years until his great moment.

Conference Report, October 1969, p. 125

He Rebuked the Waves

The Lord has endowed some individuals with a gift and capacity for possessing and exercising great powers of faith. Such a man was Henry A. Dixon. Although married and with a family of many children, when called by the First Presidency to fill a mission to Great Britain, he readily accepted the call without hesitation. With three missionary traveling companions, he embarked from St. John's in Newfoundland on the steamship Arizona.

En route a furious storm arose. As the missionaries were preparing to have their evening prayers prior to retiring, they felt a shocking jolt that caused the entire ship to quiver. As they rushed to the deck they discovered that the ship, traveling at full speed, had rammed a gigantic iceberg. A huge, gaping hole had been torn in the prow of the vessel, which extended below the water line. The captain advised that only in a calm sea could he and the crew bring the ship to the nearest port, which was 250 miles away.

The wind and the storm continued unabated. Many hours later and unable to sleep, Elder Dixon arose, dressed, and walked to the deck. Standing there alone in the dark, with deep humility and great faith, by the power of the Holy Priesthood, he rebuked the waves and commanded them to be still. Thirty-six hours later the ship was able to return and dock at St. John's. Not a single life had been lost.

When the ship's owner, a Mr. Guion, learned of the accident, and knowing that Mormon missionaries were aboard, he was quoted as saying: "There is nothing to worry about. My line has transported Mormon missionaries for forty years and has never lost a boat with Mormon missionaries aboard!"

Not only was faith a powerful force in this instance, but it is also a strong and motivating factor in the lives of numerous individuals, bringing to them comfort and peace of mind.

Conference Report, October 1970, pp. 19-20.

A. THEODORE TUTTLE

Albert Theodore Tuttle became a member of The First Council of the Seventy on April 10, 1958. From 1961 to 1965 he was president of the missions in South America, and he later supervised the Intermountain Indian Mission.

Elder Tuttle was born March 2, 1919 in Manti, Utah, a son of Albert Melvin and Clarice M. Beal Tuttle. He graduated from Manti High School and Snow College. He continued his education at Brigham Young University where he received his bachelor's degree in 1943. In 1949 he was awarded his masters degree from Stanford University.

During World War II, Elder Tuttle served nearly three years as a Marine line officer in the Pacific theater. During his military service he was also group leader for the Latter-day Saint servicemen of the Fifth Marine Division. He married Marne Whitaker on July 26, 1943 in the Manti Temple. They are the parents of seven children.

He was sustained as a member of the First Quorum of the Seventy on October 1, 1976.

Elder Tuttle passed away in Salt Lake City on November 28, 1986.

Thank You

May I share with you a personal experience? We had spent nearly four years in South America and returned just in time for our eldest son to enter Brigham Young University. Several months after school had begun we received a call—I think it was a collect call—and the conversation proceeded something like this:

"Hello, Dad?"

"Yes."

"This is David."

"Yes, what do you want now?"

"Oh, nothing."

"Nothing! Well, why did you call then?"

"Oh, I just wanted to tell you about school. I love it. It's great. I am glad to be here. I like the place where I live. I like my roommate. I like my professors and I like the spirit here."

And I said, "Yes, but what do you need?"

"I don't need anything."

"Well, why did you call?"

"I just called to say thank you. I am grateful for your helping me to be here."

Well, there was considerable silence on our end of the line and we muttered something about, "We're glad you're happy." Later that night as his mother and I prayed, we thanked the Lord for a thankful son. The lesson, of course, came clear to me. I appreciate a son who says thank you for things that parents have done, as all parents do. But I am a son also. I have a Father in heaven, who, like me, appreciates a son or a daughter who frequently says, "Thank you."

What kind of thanks?

BYU Speeches of the Year, "What Kind of Thanks," November 26, 1968, p. 4.

He Was Obviously from the Farm

There are some four thousand returned missionaries sitting here today (and a host of prospective missionaries) who ought to express appreciation to that mother who instilled a missionary spirit in her son when first she held him in her arms, and as she taught and counseled him through the years of his sometimes wavering youth. Most missionaries know that they are to go on missions before they know what a mission is, thanks to the vision and faith of their mothers.

I hope I can always remember the scene that Brother Packer and I saw several years ago. While we were waiting in the Deseret Book Company for some materials, we saw a slender young man, bronzed from exposure to the sun except for the pale border that a recent haircut revealed, purchasing his missionary supplies. He was dressed in a new suit, new shirt, new shoes, and new hat. That he was obviously from the farm was also evident from his parents who accompanied him. His father's rough, gnarled hands spoke eloquently of the years of hard, manual labor. His mother wore a tidy but faded housedress. His father's old-styled suit, frayed shirt, and run-down heels on his shoes bore mute testimony that sending their son on a mission was not going to be easy. This mother and father hovered around their son suggesting this or that book. Having purchased the standard works and his LP book and some miscellaneous things, we heard his father say, "Now, is there anything else you need, son?"

I have thought of that little episode in the lives of those three people—and it could be multiplied hundreds, and I suppose thousands of times—and I have thought, "Yes, there is something more that son needs—a grateful heart and a firm resolve to prove worthy of his heritage!"

I set a missionary apart last Wednesday, and as I handed him his missionary certificate, tears filled his eyes and he said, "Finally! I have waited nineteen years for this. Now, let me at them!"

What kind of thanks?

Take a moment for prayer and express gratitude to those who touch your life and make you better. The expression of gratitude is a divine attribute. We need to cultivate it and we need to practice it.

BYU Speeches of the Year, "What Kind of Thanks," November 26, 1968, p. 5.

A Young Boy's Answer

You have all heard the story of the young boy who fell out of bed. The next morning his grandpa was asking about it and said, "Well, young man, how come you fell out of bed?" And the boy said, "Well, I guess I didn't get in far enough." Now, my personal view is that some men who are on the outside now are there because they weren't "in far enough." Today I am appealing for a dedication to this work that has never been equaled in the past and which we must have if we are to fill that "unprecedented responsibility" that this day demands.

Talk given to Seminary and Institute Personnel, "Men With A Message," 1958.

Let It Fly Clear up to the Sky

There will be days when some discipline is needed. Let me tell you a story that illustrates why we put brakes on you, and why we sometimes hold you down.

A father was out with his son flying a kite. He had let nearly all of the string out. As the son saw the kite go higher, he said, "Dad, let it go, let it fly clear up to the sky!" This wise father, seeing an opportunity to teach a great lesson, replied, "Oh, no son. If we were to let go of the string the kite would fall down immediately. Son, remember that we have to keep a hold on it to keep it up. Sometimes the things that hold you down are the things that hold you up!"

Now sons, we love you, but we also know you. Ofttimes we know far better than you do when to hold you down, how late you are to stay out, when you are to come in, and when to do many other things. We won't deliberately make any mistakes.

Conference Report, April 1967, p. 96.

JOHN H. VANDENBERG

John H. Vandenberg was sustained as the Church's Presiding Bishop on September 30, 1961. He served in that calling for more than a decade before being sustained as an Assistant to the Twelve in 1972. He was later sustained to the First Quorum of the Seventy on October 1, 1976.

Elder Vandenberg was closely associated with the vast building program of the Church for many decades, serving as vice-chairman of the Building Committee in charge of finances.

Bishop Vandenberg was born on December 18, 1904 in Ogden, Utah, where he received his formal education. He married Ariena Stok, and they have two daughters.

Bishop Vandenberg was formerly employed in the merchandising of wool and livestock in Denver, Colorado. He was also involved in textile manufacturing and ranching.

Elder Vandenberg passed away in Sandy, Utah, on June 3, 1992.

The Most Wonderful Thing in the World

Learning comes pretty early in life. I remember as a lad, when I was about twelve years old, I was walking down the street with a friend who was not a member of the Church. This was during World War I. We heard a racket overhead. We looked and there was a biplane—a little cloth plane making a terrible racket. We looked up and admired and marveled at what was going on.

I said to my companion, "Isn't it wonderful?"

My companion said, "The most wonderful thing in the world!"

As he said that, I stopped and thought for a moment. Then I said, "No, friend, that is not the most important thing in the world. True religion is the most important thing in the world."

I suppose I had said that because of the training that I had had in Sunday School and in Primary and in my home, because I come from a home where my parents were good Latter-day Saints. And they were very desirous that their children learn of the true gospel. I suppose from birth, and being in this environment, it started to sink in.

To know that true religion is the most important thing in life, I think, has played a very important part in my life.

Speeches of the Year, "What Will You Choose," February 28, 1967, pp. 2-3.

My Dearest Father Bishopric

Sometime ago a letter came to my desk, written by a woman investigator, which carried with it a great deal of enthusiasm and testimony, and I would like to share with you tonight the following excerpts from this letter. Her salutation was this:

My dearest Father Bishopric:
You are going to be rather surprised to hear from me, but I attended Sunday services of The Church of Jesus Christ of Latter-day Saints today and was so inspired...

I owe my gratitude to just about the finest, well-cultured, and intellectual gentlemen.... They graciously invited themselves into my home and explained the Mormons.... I just had to go to church with them on the following Sunday. The book on how Joseph Smith tells his own story was so outstanding, with great love of God for each and every human being, that my knowledge of religion certainly broadened just by meeting these two elders.

On entering the church I was so astonished to see how many young people of today are attending church, and especially thrilled to see how the young mothers bring their lovely children.... The thing that touched me deeply is how the elders or brothers were so anxious just to be able to say, "How do you do?" This is something you don't see in other churches...

The Aaronic Priesthood conducted the sacrament . . . which was so pure with delight, followed by the separation to classes. At this time the elders led me to the adult class.... Here is where I accumulated knowledge in one half hour that I did not know in a lifetime of fifty years...

I also enjoyed the opening prayer, which put a dent in my mind that these are a group of people that have to be made more known in our United States of America...

Again I say how happy I was to attend services in your Mormon Latter-day Saint Church, and how mighty proud the mission must be of the elders. They are an inspiration that many mothers and fathers today can learn the message from God to his children to make this a better world to live in like God intended it to be.

As I read this thrilling letter, I thought, "What a great blessing to the elder's parents and to those missionaries, although they are unaware of the great spiritual lift that they gave to this woman."

As the woman stated, "I owe my gratitude to just about the finest, well-cultured, and intellectual gentlemen." I wondered what greater honor could there be than to be so highly esteemed by one's neighbors. No doubt this experience is happening time and time again the world over.

Conference Report, April 1962, p. 84.